Armies of the Crimean War, 1853–1856

Freepost Plus RTKE-RGRJ-KTTX
Pen & Sword Books Ltd
47 Church Street
BARNSLEY
S70 2AS

DISCOVER MORE ABOUT PEN & SWORD BOOKS

Pen & Sword Books have over 4000 books currently available, our imprints include; Aviation, Naval, Military, Archaeology, Transport, Frontline, Seaforth and the Battleground series, and we cover all periods of history on land, sea and air.

Can we stay in touch? From time to time we'd like to send you our latest catalogues, promotions and special offers by post. If you would prefer not to receive these, please tick this box. ☐

We also think you'd enjoy some of the latest products and offers by post from our trusted partners: companies operating in the clothing, collectables, food & wine, gardening, gadgets & entertainment, health & beauty, household goods, and home interiors categories. If you would like to receive these by post, please tick this box. ☐

We respect your privacy. We use personal information you provide us with to send you information about our products, maintain records and for marketing purposes. For more information explaining how we use your information please see our privacy policy at www.pen-and-sword.co.uk/privacy. You can opt out of our mailing list at any time via our website or by calling 01226 734222.

Mr/Mrs/Ms ....

Address ....

Postcode .... Email address...

Website: www.pen-and-sword.co.uk   Email: enquiries@pen-and-sword.co.uk
Telephone: 01226 734555   Fax: 01226 734438
Stay in touch: facebook.com/penandswordbooks or follow us on Twitter @penswordbooks

Armies of the Crimean War, 1853–1856

History, Organization and Equipment of the British, French, Turkish, Piedmontese and Russian Forces

Gabriele Esposito

Pen & Sword
MILITARY

First published in Great Britain in 2023
by Pen & Sword Military
An imprint of
Pen & Sword Books Limited
Yorkshire – Philadelphia

Copyright © Gabriele Esposito 2023

ISBN 978 1 39908 985 2

The right of Gabriele Esposito to be identified as
Author of this Work has been asserted by him in accordance
with the Copyright, Designs and Patents Act 1988.

A CIP catalogue record for this book is
available from the British Library

All rights reserved. No part of this book may be reproduced or
transmitted in any form or by any means, electronic or mechanical
including photocopying, recording or by any information storage and
retrieval system, without permission from the Publisher in writing.

Typeset by Mac Style
Printed and bound in India by Replika Press Pvt. Ltd.

Pen & Sword Books Limited incorporates the imprints of After the Battle,
Atlas, Archaeology, Aviation, Discovery, Family History, Fiction, History,
Maritime, Military, Military Classics, Politics, Select, Transport, True Crime,
Air World, Frontline Publishing, Leo Cooper, Remember When, Seaforth
Publishing, The Praetorian Press, Wharncliffe Local History, Wharncliffe
Transport, Wharncliffe True Crime and White Owl.

For a complete list of Pen & Sword titles please contact

PEN & SWORD BOOKS LIMITED
47 Church Street, Barnsley, South Yorkshire, S70 2AS, England
E-mail: enquiries@pen-and-sword.co.uk
Website: www.pen-and-sword.co.uk
or
PEN AND SWORD BOOKS
1950 Lawrence Rd, Havertown, PA 19083, USA
E-mail: Uspen-and-sword@casematepublishers.com
Website: www.penandswordbooks.com

Contents

Acknowledgements vii
Introduction viii

Chapter 1 The British Army 1
Chapter 2 The French Army 73
Chapter 3 The Russian Army 113
Chapter 4 The Ottoman Army 163
Chapter 5 The Piedmontese Army 179

Bibliography 195
Index 197

Gabriele Esposito is a military historian who works as a freelance author and researcher for some of the most important publishing houses in the military history sector. In particular, he is an expert specializing in uniformology: his interests and expertise range from the ancient civilizations to modern post-colonial conflicts. During recent years he has conducted and published several researches on the military history of the Latin American countries, with special attention on the War of the Triple Alliance and the War of the Pacific. He is among the leading experts on the military history of the Italian Wars of Unification and the Spanish Carlist Wars. His books and essays are published on a regular basis by Pen & Sword Books, Osprey Publishing, Winged Hussar Publishing and Libreria Editrice Goriziana, and he is also the author of numerous military history articles appearing in specialized magazines such as *Ancient Warfare Magazine*, *Medieval Warfare Magazine*, *The Armourer*, *History of War*, *Guerres et Histoire*, *Focus Storia* and *Focus Storia Wars*.

Acknowledgements

This book is dedicated to my parents, Maria Rosaria and Benedetto, for their great love and precious advice. A very special thanks goes to Philip Sidnell, the commissioning editor of my books for Pen & Sword, for his passion and for his vision. The creation of the present title would have never been possible without the hard work and excellent skills of two professionals who, by now, are also friends of mine: Matt Jones and Tony Walton. All the pictures published in this book are in the public domain, obtained from three magnificent digital archives: the Digital Collections of the New York Public Library (https://digitalcollections.nypl.org/), the Digital Repository of the Brown University Library (https://repository.library.brown.edu/studio/) and the Royal Collection Trust (https://www.rct.uk/).

Introduction

During the nineteenth century, the Ottoman Empire was considered – from a political and diplomatic point of view – as the 'sick man' of Europe, having experienced a series of significant internal difficulties. During previous centuries, the Ottomans had been one of the major military powers of the Mediterranean world thanks to the excellent performance of both their army and navy. For more than two centuries, from the fall of Constantinople in 1453 to their second siege of Vienna in 1683, the Turks had expanded their multinational empire by conquering new territories across the Mediterranean. Ottoman-controlled lands comprised a large portion of North Africa's coastline (from the eastern borders of Morocco to Egypt), the Middle East, the coastline of Arabia, the southern portion of the Caucasus and most of the southern Balkans. During the eighteenth century, the military ascendancy of Austria and Russia in Eastern Europe caused serious problems for the Turks, who had to fight several conflicts against the European powers to keep possession of their Balkan territories. Following a series of Ottoman defeats, it became clear that the Turkish state was entering a phase of long decline: the once-effective and warlike Ottoman troops became no match for European armies, which were now equipped with modern muskets and underwent regular training. Differently from the other powers of the Mediterranean, the Ottoman Empire did not participate in the 'military revolution' of the eighteenth century and thus did not modernize its old-fashioned military forces. Consequently, an obvious gap in quality came into being between Turkish soldiers and those of the major European states.

In many ways, the Ottoman Empire of the early nineteenth century was essentially still organized as a medieval Islamic state, its institutions suffering badly from corruption and nepotism. The administrative structure of Turkish territories was becoming increasingly weak due to a chronic lack of funds and the secessionist movements that were developing in various areas of the empire. Austria and Russia – keen to conquer new territories in the Balkans – supported countries like Serbia and Romania in their national uprisings against the Turks. The Balkan revolts, caused by both political and religious factors, became a massive problem for the Ottomans during the first half of the nineteenth century. The emergence of various local nationalities inside Turkish-held territories represented a major problem for the Ottomans, who had previously been able to exert a strong influence over even those lands that had retained a certain degree of autonomy since the early days of Turkish control. In the Balkans, the Turks face revolts by five different nations: Serbia, Montenegro, Greece, Moldavia and Wallachia. The latter two states had always enjoyed a high degree of autonomy, having been organized as vassal states of the Ottoman Empire that were collectively known as the Danubian Principalities. The other three states were always garrisoned by Turkish forces. During the first half of the nineteenth century, the Russians twice invaded the Danubian Principalities (in 1811 and 1828) with the objective of reaching Constantinople and thereby gaining direct access to the Mediterranean Sea at the expense of the Ottomans. Since the 1830s, the Ottomans had received strong diplomatic support from Great Britain and France, two powers with no desire to see the emergence of a strong Russian presence in the Mediterranean. On 2 July 1853, recognizing full well that the Turks were in a desperate military situation, the Russians once again invaded the Danubian Principalities, leading to the outbreak of what became known as the Crimean War. The Ottomans were defeated several times within a few months and it seemed that Russian armies were indeed going to conquer Constantinople. Alarmed by these events, Britain and France declared war on Russia in March 1854. What had been a localized conflict was thus transformed into the largest and bloodiest war fought between European powers since the days of the Napoleonic Wars. The main theatre of operations would be the Crimean peninsula in southern Ukraine, hence the conflict's name. In 1855, the anti-Russian front was also joined by the Kingdom of Sardinia, commonly known as Piedmont, the most powerful state of pre-unification Italy. As a result, five major armies started to be involved in the Crimean War. In this book we will describe in detail the main features of all the military forces that took part in this conflict, including lesser-known units that have never before been studied in English.

Chapter 1

The British Army

Guard and line infantry

All the European armies of the post-Napoleonic nineteenth century comprised a certain number of 'guard' units, which were an elite of the military forces of each country. These varied between small bodyguard corps, having a main function of merely escorting their monarch, and larger combatant units with superior training and morale. In Great Britain, the Royal Guard had a very long tradition, consisting of fighting units with a special status which performed peculiar duties. The infantry component of the British Royal Guard consisted of three regiments: the 1st Foot Guards (or Grenadier Guards), 2nd Foot Guards (Coldstream Guards) and 3rd Foot Guards (Scots Guards). The Grenadier Guards had been created in 1665, the Coldstream Guards in 1650 and the Scots Guards in 1642. The backbone of these regiments was the NCOs, professional soldiers who were able to train their men to a very high standard. It was the NCOs' duty to transform young recruits into battle-hardened veterans, thereby preserving the traditions of the unit. Obedience, endurance, loyalty and pride were the four key factors behind the elite status of the foot guards. Their uniform and equipment had to always be in perfect order, especially when performing guard duties at Windsor or St James's Palace, the principal homes of the monarch at that time. Most of the common soldiers serving in the Foot Guard regiments came from the militia and thus already had some experience of military life. Under the strict guidance of the NCOs, they were rapidly turned into professional soldiers who were able to face any combat situation. Even more important to the Foot Guards than the NCOs, however, were the officers, who gave the regiments their real and distinctive character. Most officers came from important aristocratic families of land-owners which had long military traditions. They were known as 'Gentlemen's Sons', while Wellington had called them 'fellows in silk stockings', but despite their nicknames, they time and again showed their unrivalled military competence and courage. Buying an officer's commission in the guard infantry regiments was extremely costly, limiting access to the sons of the aristocracy or the upper middle classes. Daily life in time of peace was very expensive for such officers: it was spent in the most prestigious gentlemen's clubs of London and obliged them to invest large sums of money in order to have the most elegant uniforms and be part of high society.

2   Armies of the Crimean War, 1853–1856

British privates of the Coldstream Guards photographed upon their return from the Crimean War, which was the first major conflict to receive extensive photographic coverage. They are all wearing the new M1855 double-breasted tunic introduced during the conflict and the massive bearskin headgear that was typical of the British guard infantry. The bearskin came into use in 1815 to celebrate the victory of the British foot guard regiments over the famous French Foot Grenadiers of the Imperial Guard at Waterloo (the distinctive headgear of Napoleon's foot guardsmen was the bearskin).

The three regiments of Foot Guards each had three battalions, while a single battalion comprised eight field companies and one depot company, plus a small staff. Of the field companies, two had elite status and were known as flank companies because they were deployed on the flanks of the others during combat: they were the

British sergeant of the Grenadier Guards with M1855 uniform.

Uniforms of the British Grenadier Guards (from left to right): drummer, sergeant and sapper. The musicians were very easy to recognize on the battlefield due to the additional stripes of coloured lace that they wore on the sleeves and their decorative shoulder wings. The sergeant in the centre is wearing fatigue dress, which includes dark blue pillbox cap and white waistcoat. The red waist-sash was typical of officers and NCOs. The sapper, like the drummer, is wearing the old M1846 tunic with white lace on the buttonholes that remained in use until the new 1855 dress regulations. Note his white leather apron, white leather gauntlet gloves, white badge embroidered on the sleeves and working tools (including a massive axe).

grenadier company (heavy infantry) and the light infantry company. Between 1815 and 1854, the three regiments of guard infantry did not see service overseas, but when Britain entered the Crimean War it was decided to form a temporary Brigade of the Guard for service against Russia. This brigade, which would be disbanded at the end of hostilities, consisted of the 3rd Battalion of the Grenadier Guards, the 1st Battalion of the Coldstream Guards and the 1st Battalion of the Scots Guards. Comprising veteran soldiers with great experience, the brigade performed extremely well during the conflict, distinguishing itself in battle at the Alma (1854), Inkerman (1854) and Sevastopol (1855).

British infantrymen departing for the Crimea. On the left are a sergeant and a private of the line infantry, both wearing the M1844 'Albert' shako. This headgear took its name from the Prince Consort of Queen Victoria. In the centre is a private of the Rifle Brigade with its distinctive dark green dress, while on the right is a private from a Highland regiment.

At the beginning of the Crimean War, the British line infantry comprised three regiments of fusiliers, eighty regiments of line infantry and seven regiments of Highland infantry. This general structure had not changed to any great extent since the days of the Napoleonic Wars. The three regiments of fusiliers, despite their peculiar denomination, had the same standard features as the normal line infantry, but they were some of the most ancient foot corps of the British Army. Originally, fusiliers were infantry tasked with escorting the army's artillery train, but over time they became standard line infantrymen. The regiments of fusiliers in the British Army by 1854 were the Royal Fusiliers (created in 1685), the Royal Scots Fusiliers (created in 1678) and the Royal Welch Fusiliers (created in 1689). Some of the lowest-numbered and therefore most senior line infantry regiments had three battalions each, but the majority of them consisted of just two battalions. Each of these battalions comprised eight field companies and one depot company, plus a small staff. Of the field companies, two were the flank companies of grenadiers and light infantrymen.

The Scottish regiments of the British Army could be divided into two main categories: those recruited from the Lowlands and those recruited from the Highlands. The Lowland regiments were part of the British line infantry's establishment, while the Highland units had a separate establishment and wore distinctive Scottish uniforms. The

British private of the 28th Regiment of Foot photographed in Crimea. He is wearing an M1846 tunic and pillbox cap. This was the standard appearance of the British line infantrymen during the early phases of the Crimean War.

British line infantrymen photographed soon after their arrival in Crimea. The figure on the left has the grey winter greatcoat, while those in the centre have the 'Albert' shako and M1846 tunic. The privates on the right are wearing fatigue dress.

internal organization of the Highland infantry regiments, however, was the same as the British line infantry units. Generally speaking, the Highlanders were excellent soldiers: sometimes they could be less disciplined than their English comrades, but their courage and fitness were unrivalled. They were drilled to defend a position to the last man and were extremely proud of their regimental traditions. On many occasions they were able to achieve success despite being at a distinct numerical inferiority, and their morale was usually very high. As the Highlanders were used to living in poor and rocky countryside, where conditions were extremely harsh, they could endure hardships of any kind while on campaign, being able to carry on for several days with very little food. They were able to move very rapidly on every kind of terrain, and thus had excellent skirmishing abilities. In combat, the Highlanders were prone to use their bayonets much more frequently than their English comrades, since their fighting spirit was still that of the ancient Celtic warriors; when needed, however, they could deliver very accurate fire against the enemy ranks.

British privates of the 19th Regiment of Foot in 1854, all wearing the M1844 'Albert' shako and M1846 tunic. The figure on the left is a fusilier, as indicated by the half-red and half-white pompom of his headgear. The soldier in the centre with white pompom is a grenadier, while that on the right with green pompom is from a light company. Grenadier and light infantry company uniforms had shoulder wings.

Rifles and light infantry

Most of the light infantry and rifle regiments of the British Army were created during the Napoleonic Wars, as until the beginning of the nineteenth century the British infantry comprised just a few light corps, usually recruited from foreigners. The main difference between the light infantry and rifle regiments was in their personal equipment: the light infantry were uniformed in red like the line infantry and were armed with a lighter version of the standard smoothbore musket, whereas

British officer (left) and private (right) of the 14th Regiment of Foot. They are both wearing a grey greatcoat – that was standard issue during cold months – and pillbox cap.

the riflemen wore dark green and were armed with rifled carbines that were designed specifically for them. There were two rifle regiments: the 60th Regiment of Foot and the 95th Regiment of Foot. The 60th was raised in 1756, largely as a result of a disastrous defeat suffered by the British line infantry two years beforehand at

British veterans of the 95th Regiment of Foot photographed soon after their return from Crimea. They all have the new M1855 double-breasted tunic and pillbox cap (the latter was campaign and fatigue headgear).

the Battle of Monogahela in North America during the French-Indian War. This battle saw the ambush of 1,300 British soldiers by a smaller force of French and native Indians, who annihilated their opponents. The British contingent included line infantry from the 44th Foot and 48th Foot, in addition to provincial soldiers of the Virginia Regiment commanded by a young George Washington. The clash was a disaster for the British, who lost over 450 men in the ambush, having proved unable to effectively counter their enemy's skirmishing tactics.

The new light infantry unit created after the Battle of Monogahela was initially known as the 62nd Royal American Regiment of Foot, only adopting its definitive number (the 60th) at a later date. Approval for the raising of the new regiment, as well as the necessary funds, was granted by the British Parliament in late 1755. The new unit comprised four battalions, each of 1,000 men, its main function being to oppose the raids launched by the French and their native allies against the British

British colour sergeant of the 21st Regiment of Foot with M1855 tunic and pillbox cap. Note the peculiar badge embroidered on the sleeve, which was typical of colour sergeants.

British officer (left) and private (right) of the Grenadier Guards. The officer is wearing the dark blue frock coat that was extremely popular for home service, together with the peaked cap. The private has a dark blue pillbox cap and white waistcoat.

The British Army 13

Scottish private of the 93rd Regiment of Foot, the Sutherland Highlanders, the unit made famous by the 'Thin Red Line' during the Battle of Balaclava. He is wearing M1846 dress with the typical feather bonnet of the Highland foot regiments.

Scottish officer of the 42nd Regiment of Foot, the Black Watch, photographed in Crimea. His dress includes a fatigue peaked cap, kilt, sporran bag and 'hose' socks.

Scottish veterans of the 42nd Regiment of Foot photographed soon after their return from Crimea. They are all wearing M1855 full dress with feather bonnet and kilt.

Scottish veterans of the 72nd Regiment of Foot, The Duke of Albany's Own Highlanders, photographed upon returning from Crimea. They all have the M1855 tunic and 'trews' trousers (made with the same cloth as the kilts). The figure on the right wears the bonnet that was used as campaign/fatigue headgear by the Highland units.

Scottish colour sergeant (left) and officers (right) of the 71st Regiment of Foot, MacLeod's Highlanders. This unit wore 'trews' and shakos decorated with a distinctive chequered pattern that was reproduced around the officers' peaked caps.

settlements of the Thirteen Colonies. The regiment recruited colonists who already had experience of light infantry tactics, as well as numerous foreigners who had hunting skills. In particular, the British Army was interested in recruiting German or Swiss hunters and gamekeepers, like those who were already serving in the light corps of the contemporary Prussian and French armies. To allow such experienced personnel to be signed up, Parliament passed the Commissions to Foreign Protestants Act in 1756 that permitted the recruiting of foreign officers from German states and Swiss cantons. These could be employed in the new 62nd Foot, but could not rise above the rank of lieutenant-colonel. In total, some fifty officers of the new regiment came from Germany or Switzerland. The original idea behind the formation of the unit had come from Jacques Prevost, a Swiss soldier and adventurer who was a personal friend of the Duke of Cumberland (second son of King George II). Prevost was an expert in forest warfare and one of the first to understand the combat potential of light infantry. The foreign officers of the regiment included two notable personalities: Henri Bouquet (who commanded the 1st Battalion) and Frederick Haldimand (who commanded the 2nd Battalion). Both these Swiss professional soldiers made a great contribution to the development of light infantry doctrines within the British Army. Their forward-looking ideas included the introduction of rifled muskets among the rankers. These new weapons, which had extremely long barrels and spiral grooves in the bore, had started to be produced on a small scale during the early eighteenth century. They had become popular in the American colonies thanks to the German gunsmiths who emigrated to the New World and brought these new muskets with them. During the French-Indian War, the 60th Foot fought with enormous courage during several important engagements, earning a solid reputation and its famous motto '*Celer et Audax*' (Swift and Bold).

In 1762, the British Parliament, in order to keep these soldiers in the ranks of the British Army, passed the American Protestant Soldier Naturalization Act, which offered naturalization to all those foreign officers and soldiers who had already served under the Union Jack for at least two years. The 5th Battalion of the regiment was raised in 1797 from the soldiers of a German mercenary regiment (Hompesch's Mounted Riflemen) that had recently been disbanded. A 6th Battalion was added in 1799, comprising German recruits. Finally, another two battalions were raised in 1813 for service in the Americas during the War of 1812 against the United States. These last two battalions were recruited from German and Swiss prisoners of war who had originally served Napoleon. The 60th Regiment of Foot continued to be strongly linked to the Americas after the Napoleonic Wars, and remained the British foot regiment with the highest percentage of German/Swiss rankers for several decades. With the general demobilization that followed the Battle of Waterloo, the 60th Regiment of Foot was restructured on just two battalions, whose members were all equipped with rifled carbines. With the new denomination the King's Royal Rifle Corps assumed in 1830, the unit performed garrison duties for most of the middle decades of the nineteenth century. When the Crimean War broke out, the British decided to send the other rifle regiment to the theatre of operations, the 60th Regiment remaining at home. In 1855, however, it became apparent that hostilities with Russia were to be fought on a larger scale, and the King's Royal Rifle Corps was expanded with the formation of a 3rd Battalion that was raised in Ireland.

The 95th Regiment could trace its origins back to January 1800, when several line infantry regiments of the British Army were ordered to send one captain, one lieutenant, one ensign, two sergeants, one corporal and thirty of their best privates to

Officer and soldiers of the Rifle Brigade fighting in Crimea. The officer is still wearing the old M1846 dress with three rows of buttons on the front of the tunic, while the privates already have the new M1855 uniform.

be trained as riflemen. The chosen men, the best marksmen of their respective units, made up a new independent corps of riflemen. The initial idea of the Duke of York, the then commander-in-chief of the British Army, was to train these elite soldiers as riflemen and send them back to their original units in order to act as the core for the formation of rifle companies in each line regiment. This temporary training unit was named the Experimental Corps of Riflemen and was commanded by Colonel Coote Manningham (one of the leading light infantry officers of the British Army). Manningham trained the riflemen using his innovative ideas, which were published in 1800 as the 'Regulations for the Rifle Corps formed at Blachington Barracks under the command of Colonel Manningham'. The members of the Experimental Corps of Riflemen dispensed with rigid and unthinking obedience to their orders, making them more autonomous on the battlefield and creating a special relationship based on mutual trust with their officers and NCOs. A strong new sense of comradeship was developed, with one 'soldier of merit' selected in each half-platoon who would assume command of his squad when NCOs were absent and was in a privileged position to be promoted as corporal. The Experimental Corps of Riflemen comprised just five companies, each of which was divided into two equally sized platoons, which were in turn formed from four squads. The members of each squad trained and lived together every day in order to develop a close bond that was of great use on the battlefield. Meritocracy was encouraged through every possible method, including prizes offered by the officers to the best marksmen under their command. Training of this new corps was intensive, with field exercises that were made as realistic as possible. The basic idea was to forge soldiers who could be able to think in an autonomous way and act very rapidly according to particular circumstances. Individual capabilities were fundamental in this regard, and thus only the best soldiers from the whole British infantry could be admitted into the ranks of the Experimental Corps of Riflemen. Training included moving swiftly on broken terrain, surviving with the few food resources that an enemy countryside could offer, skirmishing in the open field, penetrating the enemy's lines without being noticed, launching surprise attacks to occupy enemy outposts, scouting for larger units during an advance and acting as a rearguard to cover a retreat. From the beginning, these new riflemen were given dark green uniforms and black leather equipment.

With the progress of time, new recruits were added to what from October 1800 was termed the Rifle Corps. The unit could thus be expanded and became a battalion. In February 1801, it was transferred to the official establishment of the infantry and became a permanent formation. Then in 1802, it was officially transformed into a regiment and received the denomination of the 95th 'Rifle' Regiment. During the following years, the riflemen took part in all the most important campaigns fought

Sergeant of the King's Royal Rifle Corps, with 'Albert' shako and M1846 tunic. The tunic, with three rows of buttons on the front, had changed very little since the Napoleonic Wars.

Veterans of the Rifle Brigade photographed upon their return from the Crimea. They are all wearing the new shako and double-breasted tunic that were introduced with the M1855 dress regulations. Since their foundation, the Rifles had been dressed in dark green with black leather belt equipment in order to be less visible on the battlefield.

by the British Army, always distinguishing themselves and winning an impressive amount of medals and martial awards. Due to their superior training and morale, they were usually employed as 'special forces', accomplishing missions that seemed impossible on paper. By 1815, the establishment of the regiment consisted of three battalions. After the end of the Napoleonic Wars, the 95th Regiment retained its special status and methods of training, with the three existing battalions reorganized in 1816 as the autonomous Rifle Brigade. This was later expanded to four battalions, each of which – like those of the King's Royal Rifle Corps – comprised eight companies. The four battalions were assembled into two regiments, and overall command of the Rifle Brigade was given in 1852 to Prince Albert (consort of Queen Victoria), who strove to preserve the excellent reputation of the unit. By the outbreak of the Crimean War, the Rifle Brigade was known as The Prince Consort's Own Rifle Brigade and had been reorganized as a single regiment with two battalions, each having twelve companies. Both battalions were sent to the Crimea, where they distinguished themselves in several of the bloodiest engagements (Alma, Inkerman and Sevastopol).

The success of the 95th Regiment during the Napoleonic Wars encouraged the British high command to implement its light infantry reforms, transforming several existing line regiments into light formations. The main supporter of this process was General Sir John Moore, who was ordered by the Duke of York to retrain the 52nd Regiment of Foot and 43rd Regiment of Foot as light units. Moore was commander of the 52nd Foot and had always been one of the officers who wished to expand the light component of the British infantry. The two chosen regiments were transferred in 1803 to the training camp of the Rifles at Shorncliffe in Kent, where they trained with the 95th Regiment and were gradually transformed into a light infantry corps. This change did not affect their internal structure, which continued to be based on battalions with ten companies each, but it did influence their tactics and combat doctrine. The new light infantrymen retained their red uniforms and continued to be armed with smoothbore muskets (albeit of a special 'light' version), but learned how to fight in open order and to act as skirmishers. From this moment on, the British Army started to comprise two distinct components of light infantry: the elite riflemen, who were armed with rifled carbines and were mostly employed as 'special forces', and the light infantrymen of the converted regiments, who were equipped with smoothbore muskets but were trained as light skirmishers. In September 1805, the retraining of the 43rd Foot and 52nd Foot was completed and both units were later sent to the Iberian Peninsula, where together with most of the 95th Rifles and some allied units they formed the elite Light Division that acted as a special corps for Wellington. Following the operational success of the 43rd Foot and 52nd Foot, more line infantry units were transformed into light regiments during the Napoleonic Wars by undergoing special training sessions. By 1815, the following regiments of the British infantry had become specialist 'light' ones: the 51st in 1809, the 68th in 1808, the 71st in 1809, the 85th in 1808 and the 90th in

1815. During the post-Napoleonic period, no further line infantry regiments were transformed into light units, so by 1854 there were seven regiments of light infantry in the British Army. These were organized exactly like the line infantry regiments, with eight active companies and one depot company, but were specifically trained to fight in open order and to skirmish. As had happened during the Peninsular War, a temporary Light Division was formed within the British expeditionary forces fighting against the Russians during the Crimean War. This, however, was 'light' in name only, since it consisted of the following line formations: the 33rd Regiment of Foot, Royal Welch Fusiliers and 7th Regiment of Foot in the I Brigade; and the 77th Regiment of Foot, 88th Regiment of Foot and 19th Regiment of Foot in the II Brigade. The division also included one field battery of foot artillery and one troop of horse artillery.

During the Balaclava campaign in the Crimea, the order of battle of the British infantry was as follows:

1st Infantry Division
Guards Brigade
3rd Battalion of the Grenadier Guards
1st Battalion of the Coldstream Guards
1st Battalion of the Scots Guards

Highland Brigade
42nd Highland Regiment
79th Highland Regiment

4th Infantry Division
I Brigade
20th Regiment of Foot
21st Regiment of Foot
57th Regiment of Foot
98th Regiment of Foot

II Brigade
63rd Regiment of Foot
46th Regiment of Foot
1st Battalion of the Rifle Brigade

93rd Highland Regiment (performing garrison duties)

The 93rd Highland Regiment fought with enormous courage, as did the other Highland formations, during the Battle of Balaclava (25 October 1854). The soldiers of the regiment, some 500 in total, formed the famous 'Thin Red Line' that repulsed a charge by 2,500 Russian cavalrymen without any artillery support. The Highland Brigade performed extremely well throughout the Balaclava campaign, which was unsurprising as it consisted of two Highland regiments with long-lasting military traditions. The 42nd Regiment, the oldest of the Highland units, was raised as early as 1725 as the Independent Highland Companies and fought during the Napoleonic Wars and earlier eighteenth-century conflicts in all the major engagements of the British Army. Collectively known as the Black Watch because of the dark colour of the tartan from which their kilts were made, the soldiers of the 42nd Regiment were 'crack' troops.

Guard and heavy cavalry

Like all the major European forces of the nineteenth century, the British Army contained cavalry units that had specialist 'guard' status. These acted as the mounted bodyguard of the royal family and were considered to be the elite of the British heavy cavalry. In 1854, the British guard cavalry comprised the 1st Regiment of Life Guards, the 2nd Regiment of Life Guards and the Royal Horse Guards. The two units of Life Guards were created during the late seventeenth century as four independent troops of mounted bodyguards, which were made up of young aristocrats from the most important noble families of England. Since their foundation, the Life Guards had a distinctive 'heavy cavalry' nature, and they eventually had two troops of horse grenadiers attached to them. In 1746, the 3rd Troop of Life Guards and 4th Troop of Life Guards were disbanded following the Jacobite Rebellion in Scotland and parts of northern England. In 1788, as part of the great organizational changes that took place after the British defeat in the American Revolution, it was decided to merge the two remaining troops of Life Guards with the two existing troops of Horse Grenadiers in order to form two consolidated regiments: the 1st Regiment of Life Guards and the 2nd Regiment of Life Guards. The former comprised the 1st Troop of Life Guards and 1st Troop of Horse Grenadiers, while the latter was made up from the 2nd Troop of Life Guards and 2nd Troop of Horse Grenadiers. With this important organizational change, the nature of the Life Guards also altered, the two new regiments starting to comprise ordinary soldiers – as had already happened in the troops of horse grenadiers – and no longer being made up only of young 'gentlemen'. Most of the aristocrats who were still serving in the Life Guards were pensioned off, the two new units thereafter containing soldiers who had distinguished themselves through their valour and discipline.

The Royal Horse Guards, commonly known as The Blues because of their distinctive dark blue uniforms, had a completely different history from the two regiments of Life Guards (which were dressed in red). In 1650, while Oliver Cromwell was at the peak of his power following the execution of Charles I, a heavy cavalry unit known as the Regiment of Cuirassiers was raised by Sir Arthur Haselrig. This corps had a distinct elite status from the outset and was mostly employed for escort and policing duties, essentially carrying out the same functions as the French Gendarmerie. With the Restoration of Charles II in 1660, the Regiment of Cuirassiers was transferred to royal service, most of its officers (who were still loyal to the Parliamentarian cause) being replaced by new ones who were loyal to the Stuarts. The unit initially consisted of just three troops, whose members were mostly wealthy gentlemen. By the outbreak of the Glorious Revolution in 1688, however, it had eight troops and had received the new official denomination of The King's Regiment of Horse. Shortly before the outbreak of the Glorious Revolution, the regiment received 'guard' status, but when William of Orange disembarked in England its members abandoned James II and sided with the Dutch pretender to the English throne.

During the early decades of the eighteenth century, the regiment continued to serve mostly as a police corps, garrisoning several areas of Britain and preventing the outbreak of local rebellions. In 1743, following Britain's involvement in the Austrian War of Succession that ravaged continental Europe, the regiment fought with distinction at the Battle of Dettingen. The British army that was sent across the English Channel to fight against France comprised, for the first time, a Household Brigade: this was made up of elements from the Life Guards and the Horse Grenadiers, as well as from the future Royal Horse Guards. The Blues were renamed the Regiment of Royal Horse Guards in 1750, under which they fought in the Seven Years' War. In 1788, after spending several years patrolling the East Midlands, the Royal Horse Guards were transferred to London as a result of the reorganization of the Life Guards. In 1812, the Blues contributed to the formation of the Household Brigade, together with the Life Guards, and were sent to the Iberian Peninsula to fight with Wellington. In 1814, along with the rest of the Peninsular Army, the Royal Horse Guards returned to Britain, but they were soon remobilized together with the other units of the Household Brigade following Napoleon's return to France from exile. The Blues participated with great distinction at the Battle of Waterloo, during which they fought against the French heavy cavalry. The Royal Horse Guards counter-charged against the French cuirassiers, who were considered the best heavy cavalry in Europe, with the Blues showing they were second-to-none in terms of courage and discipline, confirming their excellent reputation. In 1820, the Royal Horse Guards became formally part of the Household Cavalry and thus started to

British officer of the 1st Regiment of Life Guards. The guard cavalry of the British Army had adopted metal cuirasses after admiring the courage of the French cuirassiers during the Battle of Waterloo.

The British Army 27

British superior officer (left) and trooper of the Royal Horse Guards (right). The Royal Horse Guards have always been dressed in dark blue in order to differentiate themselves from the Life Guards, hence their nickname of 'The Blues'.

enjoy a series of privileges deriving from their new special status. In 1821, like the Life Guards, they received new uniforms, with cuirasses that were quite similar to the ones still worn today. The British had been greatly impressed by the combat capabilities of the French cuirassiers during the Battle of Waterloo, so decided to give cuirasses to their own elite heavy cavalry. The Life Guards and Horse Guards did not participate in the Crimean War, remaining at home to perform their usual duties of internal security.

At the outbreak of the Crimean War, the British heavy cavalry consisted of two distinct categories of units: the Dragoon Guards and the Dragoons, the former comprising heavy horsemen and the latter medium horsemen. However, in practice there was very little difference between the two categories since both were trained and equipped to act as 'shock' cavalry. The Dragoon Guards were created in 1746, when the general organization of the British heavy cavalry underwent a radical reform. The first two heavy cavalry units that received this new denomination were the Queen's Own Regiment of Horse and the Earl of Peterborough's Regiment of Horse, which became respectively the 1st Dragoon Guards and 2nd Dragoon Guards. In 1747, a third unit, the Earl of Plymouth's Regiment of Horse, was converted into a further regiment of Dragoon Guards. This was followed by another four such units in 1788, when the British cavalry was again reorganized; as a result, by 1854, the British Army included a total of seven regiments of Dragoon Guards.

Since the days of the Restoration (1660), the English heavy cavalry had comprised horse regiments and dragoon regiments, the former being true heavy cavalry equipped with cuirasses until the late seventeenth century, while the latter were originally raised as mounted infantry units that were not tasked with conducting battlefield charges. Initially, dragoons were introduced in many European armies from 1648 onwards as chosen units of infantry who used horses to travel long distances or to move on the battlefield but then dismounted to fight. In practice, they consisted of infantrymen with a higher degree of mobility, being armed with long infantry muskets but wearing the same leather boots as the cavalrymen of the horse regiments. Over time, notably during the early eighteenth century, the dragoons gradually lost their original mounted infantry nature and transformed themselves into regular line cavalry. At the same time, the horse regiments discarded their metal cuirasses and started to use lighter personal equipment. As a result of these changes, the original tactical differences that distinguished the horse regiments from the dragoons practically ceased to exist. Neither the heavy horsemen nor the dragoons now wore cuirasses, and both were now employed to perform the same duties. As a result, in 1746, the British government decided to transform the horse regiments into dragoon units in order to cut costs and to eliminate a nominal tactical differentiation that no

The British Army

British officer of a dragoon guards regiment, with the M1843 brass helmet typical of such units.

longer existed in practice. The heavy mounts of the horse regiments had a considerable cost but produced no real advantage on the field of battle, while the soldiers of the horse regiments had the privilege of being paid much more than the dragoons. With the creation of the Dragoon Guards, the British government found a good compromise: the costly horse regiments were abolished, but at the same time their members kept alive the glorious traditions of the British heavy cavalry. The term 'Guards' of their new official denomination underlined that the Dragoon Guards were the elite of the British heavy cavalry and marked a formal difference between them and the regular dragoons. However, the transformation of the horse regiments into Dragoon Guards was very unpopular among the units affected by it, since it led to drastic reductions in pay. Furthermore, their new official name did not signify the inclusion of the former horse regiments into the Royal Household. In practice, the Dragoon Guards were placed somewhere between the Life Guards/Horse Guards and the normal regiments of dragoons.

By the outbreak of the war with Russia, there were just three regular dragoon regiments (many of the existing regiments of dragoons had been transformed into light dragoon regiments). Consequently, the whole heavy cavalry of the British Army comprised a total of ten regiments. The Dragoon Guard formations were mostly employed to perform garrison duties around the British Isles, while the regiments of Dragoons were often sent overseas. However, the uniforms worn by the

British trooper of the 5th Dragoon Guards Regiment photographed upon his return from the Crimea. He is wearing the new M1847 'Albert' helmet.

British officer of the 5th Dragoon Guards Regiment photographed in Crimea while wearing campaign dress. He has removed the falling plume from his 'Albert' helmet and has covered his headgear with a white protective cover.

two categories of heavy cavalry were very similar. All the heavy cavalry regiments of the British Army, be they Dragoon Guards or Dragoons, were structured on troops, two of which made up a squadron. Squadrons were known by letters, with troops known by numbers. Each regiment had eight troops and thus four squadrons. One of the squadrons, known as the depot squadron, provided new recruits with some solid basic training for the three active squadrons in order to replenish the losses suffered during subsequent campaigns. The Life Guards and Horse Guards had the same internal organization as the line heavy cavalry regiments, with four squadrons. When Britain became involved in the Crimean War, an entire temporary cavalry division was formed to be sent overseas; this comprised one brigade of heavy cavalry and one of light cavalry. The Heavy Brigade consisted of the following units: the

4th Regiment of Dragoon Guards, 5th Regiment of Dragoon Guards, 1st Regiment of Dragoons, 2nd Regiment of Dragoons and 6th Regiment of Dragoons. All the regiments of dragoons of the British Army, three in total, were part of the Heavy Brigade. There was a gap in the progressive numbering, since the 3rd Regiment and 4th Regiment had been transformed into units of light dragoons (in 1818), while the 5th Regiment had been disbanded following a mutiny during the Irish Rebellion of 1798 and was re-raised only in 1858. The Heavy Brigade deployed in Crimea, like the other units of the British Army, performed very well on several occasions but did not have the opportunity to show on the battlefield its potential as a shock force.

Light cavalry

Until 1745, the British Army comprised only heavy cavalry units (horse regiments) and medium cavalry units (dragoon regiments). In that year, however, the Jacobite Rebellion began in Scotland. During this major uprising, the British cavalry experienced some difficulties in chasing the highly mobile insurgent forces of the Scots, who moved very rapidly on the broken terrain of the Highlands and were masters in employing 'hit-and-run' tactics. Consequently, the Duke of Kingston, one of the English nobles who supported the British efforts against the Jacobites, raised a volunteer horse regiment with light cavalry training from his lands in Nottinghamshire. This new corps, organized by the duke at his own expense, was officially ranked as the 10th Regiment of Horse of the British Army, its members being trained as light cavalry despite being equipped and uniformed like standard heavy horsemen. The Duke of Kingston's Regiment of Horse performed extremely well during the Jacobite Rebellion and participated in the decisive Battle of Culloden, after which it pursued the defeated Jacobites with great determination. The regulars of the British Army initially had many prejudices about this new light cavalry corps, but combat experience showed them the potential of this new kind of unit. After the end of the Jacobite Rebellion, in 1746, the 'experimental' volunteer regiment raised by the Duke of Kingston was disbanded, its members having only enlisted for the duration of the war.

The Duke of Cumberland, who had commanded the British forces at Culloden, had a very positive opinion of the unit and would have preferred to retain it in service. Although this was not possible for practical reasons, the Duke found a way to maintain some light cavalry in his forces, organizing a new light cavalry unit, known as the Duke of Cumberland's Regiment of Light Dragoons, in which he enlisted all the men of the recently disbanded Duke of Kingston's Regiment of Horse. This new corps was the first regular light cavalry unit ever formed by the British Army and the first to be ranked as Light Dragoons. In 1749, however, the Duke of Cumberland's Regiment of Light Dragoons was disbanded, and until 1757 the British cavalry continued to be made up only of horse regiments and dragoon regiments. Yet it was just a matter of time before Britain became involved in a new conflict and once again needed formations of light mounted troops. In April 1757, following the outbreak of the Seven Years' War, the founding of eleven independent troops of light cavalry was authorized, each of which was to be attached to one of the existing horse regiments. Members of these new troops were chosen from the youngest and fittest recruits of the existing horse regiments, were mounted on small and nimble horses and were trained to act as skirmishers and explorers. Thus was born the glorious tradition of the British Light Dragoons. Indeed, within a few years the new light cavalry showed their great potential, to the extent that it was decided in 1759 to form seven completely independent regiments of light cavalry. These formations were recruited very rapidly and were numbered in progressive order after the fourteen regiments of dragoons that existed at the time. By 1785, following the operational success of the light dragoons during the American Revolution, the British cavalry comprised a total of thirteen light regiments (numbered 7–19, in progressive order after the regiments of dragoons). The beginning of the long wars fought against Revolutionary and Napoleonic France increased the need for more light cavalry corps, so the number of light dragoon units was increased in 1803 from thirteen to nineteen. Following the end of the Napoleonic Wars, between 1817 and 1820, the six new regiments created during wartime were disbanded. In 1818, however, two regiments of dragoons (the 3rd and 4th) were transformed into light dragoon units.

By 1820, there had been an important diversification inside the British light cavalry, its regiments no longer all being of light dragoons. Combat experience from the Napoleonic Wars had led to the introduction of two new troop types in the cavalry of the British Army: hussars and lancers. During the early years of the Napoleonic Wars, French hussars had obtained a series of brilliant successes and became famous for their incredible courage as well as for their ornate uniforms. The British Army also fell victim to the fashion for French-style hussars, and during 1806/07 some of its light dragoon regiments were transformed into hussars. In total, four units were transformed: the 7th, 10th, 15th and 18th Light Dragoons. In 1818, the 8th Light Dragoons also became a hussar regiment, followed by the 11th Light Dragoons in 1840. The transformation of these units did not affect their training and tactical functions, nor their progressive number, but simply saw the introduction of new and much more costly hussar-style uniforms. Shortly after the Battle of Waterloo, during which British officers were impressed by the combat capabilities of the French lancers, four units of light dragoons were transformed into lancer units: the 9th,

British officers of the 3rd Light Dragoons Regiment. The figure on the left is protecting his shako with a black oilskin cover designed for campaign use.

12th, 16th and 19th Regiments. These were all retrained in the use of the cavalry lance in 1816 and were given Polish-style uniforms copied from those worn by the Napoleonic French lancers. In 1821, the 19th Regiment was disbanded, but another regiment of light dragoons, the 17th, was transformed into a unit of lancers in 1822.

As a result of the organizational changes described above, by the outbreak of the Crimean War the British light cavalry no longer consisted only of light dragoons and now included the following fourteen regiments: four of light dragoons (the 3rd, 4th, 13th and 14th), six of hussars (the 7th, 8th, 10th, 11th, 15th and 18th) and four of lancers (the 9th, 12th, 16th and 17th). The dragoons, light dragoons, hussars and lancers all had their regiments numbered in progressive order, which is why some numbers (the 1st, 2nd and 6th) were not used for the light cavalry. All the light cavalry regiments of the British Army were structured on troops, two of which made

British veterans of the 4th Light Dragoons Regiment photographed upon their return from the Crimea.

up a squadron. Squadrons were known by letters, troops by numbers. Each regiment had eight troops/four squadrons. The depot squadron provide basic training for new recruits to the three active squadrons to replenish any losses they suffered.

As stated above, an entire temporary cavalry division was formed to be sent overseas when Britain became involved in the Crimean War. This division had a

British officer of the 13th Light Dragoons Regiment wearing fatigue dress; note the golden embroidering (showing rank) on the peaked cap and jacket.

brigade of heavy cavalry and one of light cavalry. The Light Brigade consisted of the 4th Regiment of Light Dragoons, 8th Regiment of Hussars, 11th Regiment of Hussars, 13th Regiment of Light Dragoons and 17th Regiment of Lancers. The Light Brigade took part in the most iconic action of the Crimean War, the Charge of the Light Brigade (or 'Charge of the 600') that took place on 25 October 1854 during the Battle of Balaclava. This saw the brave British light cavalry launch a frontal attack against well-fortified Russian field batteries; it was a suicide action, the result of a misunderstanding in communicating orders. The Light Brigade, after advancing across what became known as the 'Valley of Death', managed to capture the Russian guns in their entrenched positions, but the exhausted British troopers – many of them wounded – were soon forced to retreat after the Russians mounted a counter-attack with their Cossacks. At the end of the action, 278 British cavalrymen had been killed, wounded or captured. General Pierre Bosquet, a French

The British Army 37

British officer of the 9th Lancers Regiment. The *czapska* headgear, here worn with a protective oilskin cover, was typically Polish.

British officer of the 12th Lancers Regiment. Here it is possible to admire the splendour of the magnificent *czapska* headgear as it was worn on parade.

British trooper of the 17th Lancer Regiment, the unit that was part of the Light Brigade and that charged at Balaclava. The motto of the regiment was 'Death or Glory' and its badge consisted of a skull placed over two crossbones (which is visible on the shabraque).

divisional commander at Balaclava, gave the following evaluation of the action: 'It is magnificent, but it is not war. It is madness.' The Light Brigade had proven its courage in launching a charge that had never been ordered, the result of rashness among some of their superior officers, and in so doing had written a glorious page in British military history.

British veterans of the 17th Lancer Regiment photographed soon after their return from the Crimea. The new double-breasted tunic shown here had replaced the old model (very similar to the one used by the light dragoons) since 1855.

British officer of the 11th Hussar Regiment photographed in Crimea while wearing full dress.

British officer of the 8th Hussar Regiment. The uniforms worn by the hussars, which had changed little since the days of the Napoleonic Wars, were the most ornate and expensive in the whole British Army.

British trumpeter of the 11th Hussar Regiment. This unit's dress was very easy to identify since it comprised cherry-coloured breeches.

Artillery and technical corps

Until 1716, with the creation of the Royal Artillery, the British Army did not have any permanent artillery formations: temporary artillery trains were previously organized by the Ordnance Department only when needed, and were usually disbanded at the end of each campaign. In time of peace, only a few dozen professional gunners were at the service of the Ordnance Department, scattered across Britain and manning the guns of the various garrisons. When war broke out, they were assembled to form an artillery train and were supplemented with a number of civilian mattrosses and pioneers, semi-skilled labourers who were contracted only for the duration of a campaign. The drivers of the carts that were used to move the artillery pieces were also all civilians. With the creation of the Royal Artillery, the eighteenth century was a period of great change and of progressive professionalization for the British Army's artillery and the smaller technical corps that supported it. The first two permanent companies/batteries of artillery of the British Army were organized in 1716 and structured as independent corps. They received the official denomination of Royal Artillery in 1720, but in practice they were an autonomous military force since their creation. The original two companies were soon increased to four, and were assembled – from an administrative point of view – with the artillery companies that had garrisoned Gibraltar and Menorca in the Mediterranean since the end of the War of the Spanish Succession. As a result of these organizational changes, the Royal Regiment of Artillery was created in 1722. This had the numerical consistency of a single battalion, and its members quickly became famed for their personal preparation and professionalism. From the outset, selection and promotion in the Royal Artillery were based on merit, and thus the officer corps of this new branch of service comprised only those who excelled in their craft. In 1741, in order to improve the general quality of all the artillerymen serving across the British Empire, a cadet company was formed at the Royal Military Academy of Woolwich, tasked with training not only the officers of the Royal Artillery Regiment but also those artillery officers who served with the British East India Company.

In 1757, the Royal Artillery Regiment was reorganized on two battalions with twelve companies each, but its expansion continued during the following decades. By 1780, it comprised the following sub-units: four active battalions with eight companies each, two 'invalid' independent companies employed to perform garrison duties and a permanent military band. By 1803, the Royal Artillery consisted of eight battalions, each with ten companies/batteries; a 9th Battalion was raised in 1806 and a 10th Battalion in 1808. The various battalions were not employed in the field as complete units, their companies/batteries usually being deployed as autonomous corps. When this happened, they were commonly known as brigades despite comprising companies

British sergeant of the Royal Artillery, photographed near a field piece and bearing the guidon of his battery. The foot artillerymen were dressed very similarly to the line infantry, but in their distinctive dark blue colour with red facings. This NCO has the fatigue/campaign pillbox cap.

with just six pieces each. Attached to each brigade there was always a detachment of artillery drivers, tasked with moving the guns in the field. After the end of the Napoleonic Wars, the expansion of the Royal Artillery Regiment continued with the formation of another two battalions, and by the time of the Crimean War the British foot artillery consisted of twelve autonomous battalions. Each of these was still structured on eight companies/batteries. A single battery comprised five guns and one howitzer. These were transported together with their limbers and various wagons that were essential for their functioning: eight ammunition wagons, three

British veteran gunners of the Royal Artillery photographed soon after their return from the Crimea. They all have pillbox cap and the new M1855 double-breasted tunic.

baggage wagons and one spare-wheel wagon. In addition, each artillery company/battery had a field forge for repairing damaged pieces.

Generally speaking, the foot artillery moved very slowly on the battlefield and changed position very rarely. This led, from the end of the eighteenth century, to the Royal Artillery Regiment starting to include a horse artillery component. The British Army was quite slow in forming its own first units of horse artillery, with two troops of this new branch of service organized only in January 1793. It is interesting

The British Army 47

British officer of the Horse Artillery Brigade, wearing full dress uniform. Since its foundation, the Horse Artillery had always been uniformed quite similarly to the light dragoons and hussars.

to note that, differently from the foot artillery, the batteries of the horse artillery were known as troops and not as companies. The internal organization of the new mounted batteries always remained similar to that of the cavalry troops, and this was also apparent in the uniforms worn by the horse artillery, which were of clear 'light cavalry' cut. Another two troops of horse artillery were organized in November 1793, and by 1801 the number of horse batteries in the British Army had been increased to seven. During the Napoleonic Wars, the number of mounted batteries reached a maximum of twelve, but after the end of the hostilities these were reduced to eight, all assembled into a single Horse Artillery Brigade. The gunners of these units were mounted on horses, while the drivers sat on the carriages or limbers of the guns when their batteries were being moved. Each horse battery was equipped with five light guns and one howitzer, except for one that was entirely equipped with rockets (which had started to be employed on a regular basis by the Royal Artillery since 1813). The foot batteries of the British artillery had 12-pdr guns and 5.5cm howitzers, while the mounted batteries had lighter 9-pdr guns and 4.5cm howitzers.

The Corps of Engineers, like the Royal Artillery, was organized as a permanent unit only in 1716. Until then, the British Army had included only a few independent officers with specific engineering skills. The formation of an independent Corps of Engineers (a 'Royal' prefix was added in 1787), however, did not significantly change the existing situation: indeed, by the outbreak of the Napoleonic Wars the Corps of Royal Engineers still comprised just a handful of commissioned officers who had undergone technical training. In 1792 there had been seventy-three of them, a number that was progressively augmented so that by 1813 the Corps of Royal Engineers mustered a total of 262 officers. They received higher pay when serving overseas and were consulted only when strictly needed, for example to conduct siege operations or build military infrastructure such as bridges. This situation did not change between 1815 and 1854, so that by the outbreak of the Crimean War the Royal Engineers was still a corps of specialist officers. The labour force for the Royal Engineers was provided by the Royal Sappers and Miners, a small technical corps consisting of twelve companies of military workers that was organized along modern lines by Wellington in 1812. The Royal Sappers and Miners performed a series of auxiliary tasks that were absolutely fundamental to the British Army in the field, which included building and carpentry. Since 1812, the soldiers of the Royal Sappers and Miners had been commanded by the commissioned officers of the Royal Engineers.

In 1793, the British Army decided to militarize its artillery drivers, who had previously been unreliable civilian contractors with no discipline and training to speak of. As a result, the new Corps of Royal Artillery Drivers was formed, comprising

Uniforms of the British Royal Engineers and Royal Sappers and Miners. The three figures on the left, from the Royal Sappers and Miners, are dressed very similarly to the line infantry, with 'Albert' shako and M1855 tunic. The sergeant has a distinctive red sash around the waist, while the musician has a dark blue frontal plastron decorated with golden lace. The officer of the Royal Engineers on the right has peaked cap and a simple dark blue frock coat, which was quite popular for campaign use. The figures in the centre, from the Royal Sappers and Miners, all have dark blue peaked caps and red stable jackets. The instrument that they are using is a sextant for land surveys.

not only soldiers but also the draught animals and the wagons that were needed to transport artillery guns and materials. By 1808, the Corps of Royal Artillery Drivers, whose members were dressed similarly to the soldiers of the horse artillery, comprised a total of eight troops. Each of the troops – commanded by a captain – deployed 450 drivers organized into five sections of ninety men each, 104 assorted craftsmen, 945 draught horses and seventy-five riding horses. By the end of the Napoleonic Wars, the Corps of Royal Artillery Drivers had been expanded to eleven troops, with a total of eighty-eight officers and 7,352 other ranks. The sections of the artillery drivers' troops were divided among the artillery companies, with one section usually attached to each battery. Wellington was never particularly happy with his Corps of Royal Artillery Drivers, whose members sometimes lacked discipline and were not guided by expert officers. Consequently, the Corps of Royal Artillery Drivers was temporarily absorbed into the Royal Artillery in 1817 before being disbanded in 1822. In addition to the Corps of Royal Artillery Drivers, the British Army of the Napoleonic Wars also had the Royal Waggon Train that was tasked with transporting all those materials of the army that did not belong to the artillery. This unit was organized in 1798, mostly with men drafted from the cavalry, and initially consisted of just three troops. Each of these troops comprised three sergeants, three corporals, one trumpeter, three artificers and sixty-two privates. During the Napoleonic Wars, the Royal Waggon Train was progressively expanded, and by 1814 was structured on fourteen troops with around 1,900 men. Generally speaking, like their equivalents in the Royal Artillery, the drivers of the Royal Waggon Train were not noted for their discipline and efficiency. In 1818, the corps was reduced to just two troops, and was completely disbanded in 1833. As a result, when the Crimean War broke out, the British Army had no train units that could transport its materials on campaign. This caused serious problems during the early months of fighting against the Russians, to the point that in January 1855 it was decided to form a new Royal Transport Corps as the heir to the Royal Waggon Train. The new branch of service, which became known as the Royal Train in 1856, consisted of seven regiments with two battalions

Contemporary print showing the British Mounted Staff Corps embarking for Crimea. The uniform of this small military police corps was extremely elegant: black 'Albert' helmet with black horsehair mane, red hussar jacket with black frontal frogging and dark blue trousers with red side-stripes.

each. The whole corps had a distinct 'cavalry' nature during the early phase of its history; each train battalion, for example, was structured on three squadrons.

Among the technical formations of the British Army that took part in the Crimean War we should also mention the Mounted Staff Corps, a temporary military police unit that was created following the example of Wellington's Staff Corps of Cavalry. The Mounted Staff Corps was raised soon after the outbreak of hostilities with Russia and consisted of fifty policemen who were mostly recruited from the Irish Constabulary. The unit was a provost corps tasked with enforcing discipline among British soldiers who operated overseas. The military policemen were intended to prevent desertion and looting, but were also required to perform other auxiliary duties. They received extra pay for their services and wore a distinctive uniform. The Mounted Staff Corps, however, did not perform particularly well and was disbanded in the autumn of 1855. Some months later, a new attempt to organize a military police force – this time a permanent one – was made by the British. A total of just twenty-one NCOs and troopers, coming from different cavalry units, were embodied to form the new Military Mounted Police Corps, tasked with preserving good order in the large military camp that had been built at Aldershot to train militia units mobilized during the Crimean War. After the end of hostilities, this unit continued to exist and was progressively expanded, later becoming the Military Police of the British Army.

Royal Marines and Royal Marine Artillery

Until 1755, the naval infantry component of the Royal Navy was provided by several infantry regiments that were detached from the rest of the British Army for service at sea. This practice of using regular infantry units to perform naval infantry duties had begun in 1664, when the Duke of York and Albany's Maritime Regiment of Foot was raised; also known as the Admiral's Regiment, it provided infantrymen to several warships of the English Navy. In 1755, the British government decided to organize an independent corps of naval infantry, which received the official denomination of Marines (changed to Royal Marines only in 1802). The new naval infantry was initially structured on fifteen autonomous companies, each of which could be sent to serve on a particular warship. Unlike the sailors of the Royal Navy, the Marines were all volunteers, like the infantrymen of the British Army, and thus had a lot in common with them (including their red uniforms). The various companies of Marines were assembled administratively into three divisions that took their name from the location where they were based: Chatham, Portsmouth and Plymouth. In 1805, a fourth division was established at Woolwich. Each of these divisions

Uniforms of the British Royal Marines (from left to right): colour sergeant, private and drummer. The Royal Marines were dressed similarly to the line infantry, with red tunics and dark blue trousers.

comprised a different number of companies. By 1854, there were 110 companies of Royal Marines, each having around 100 soldiers each. The Royal Marines played a key role during the Crimean War, supporting the British Army on several occasions by fighting as normal line infantry. Once the British expeditionary force reached the theatre of operations, for example, 1,200 Royal Marines were ordered to leave their warships. They were assembled together to form a temporary Royal Marines

British veterans of the Royal Marine Artillery photographed soon after their return from the Crimea. The Royal Marine Artillery was dressed quite similarly to the Royal Artillery, with dark blue tunics and trousers.

Battalion that fought as a regular foot unit against the Russians. The naval infantry's normal tasks, however, were acting as marksmen on warships, conducting boarding operations, manning the guns of warships on which they served and organizing amphibious landings. In addition, they were tasked with preventing or crushing any mutinies that took place among the sailors of a warship. In December 1854, the Royal Navy further contributed to the war efforts in Crimea by landing 1,000 of its officers and sailors. These were asked to operate as normal infantrymen or artillerymen and were assembled into a temporary Naval Brigade. This was equipped with heavy naval guns taken from the warships, but was often employed as an infantry unit (a role in which it performed well). The practice of forming temporary battalions of Royal Marines and brigades of sailors remained common in the British armed forces until the First World War. Prior to 1804, the guns of the Royal Navy's warships were manned by the Royal Marines or by the sailors embarked on each vessel. However, this sometimes caused serious difficulties since a specific level of competence was needed to effectively fire the guns of a warship. Consequently, in August of that year, a new corps called the Royal Marine Artillery was formed, although it was officially only known as such from 1859. This was part of the Royal Marines, but its members were naval artillerymen and not naval infantry. By 1854, the Royal Marine Artillery was structured on twelve companies, its members uniformed in dark blue rather than red like the Royal Marines (despite being part of the latter). In January 1855, the Royal Marines assumed the new denomination of Royal Marines Light Infantry, which was amended to Royal Marine Light Infantry in 1862; the change of name, however, did not affect the organization of the corps.

Colonial military units

In 1854, Great Britain already controlled the largest colonial empire in the world, comprising territorial possessions distributed around all the continents. Some of the British colonies, such as Australia or New Zealand, were garrisoned by regular units of the British Army that were sent to serve overseas, along with militia units recruited on a local basis. Other colonies, like Canada or South Africa, had their own local regular units that were charged with the defence of the territory. India was controlled by the East India Company, and thus had its own independent armed forces, which will be covered in a separate section below. In the Americas, Britain had the large colony of Canada plus several smaller territories located inside or around the Caribbean, commonly known as the West Indies. When the Crimean War broke out, Canada still bordered Russian Alaska, which was only sold to the United States in 1867. However, since most of north-western Canada had not yet been explored and colonized by 1854, no military operations took place along the border between British Canada and Russian Alaska. The most important local regular unit garrisoning Canada was the Royal Canadian Rifle Regiment, which had been raised in 1840 from veterans of the British Army who had served in Canada and lived in the country. To be part of the unit, fifteen years of good service in the British Army were an essential requirement, meaning the regiment comprised very experienced soldiers. Members of the Royal Canadian Rifle Regiment enjoyed a series of privileges: they received double pay, could be pensioned upon completing twenty-one years of military service and were given a free grant of land upon retirement. The unit was divided into a series of small detachments which were scattered across the whole territory of Canada. The Royal Canadian Rifle Regiment had a lot in common with the British 60th Regiment of Foot, being a unit whose members wore the same dark green uniforms as the 60th and were all armed with rifled carbines. Being elite riflemen trained to fight in the North American forests, the soldiers of the regiment enjoyed a high reputation. The regular garrison of Canada also comprised three independent companies of line infantry, known as the Royal Newfoundland Companies. These were mostly made up of former servicemen who were ex-patients of the Royal Hospital for Invalid Soldiers of Chelsea. These veterans were tasked with garrisoning the large Atlantic island of Newfoundland. In 1842, the Royal Newfoundland Companies were formally attached to the Royal Canadian Rifle Regiment.

By the beginning of the nineteenth century, the islands of the West Indies formed one of the most economically profitable areas of the world. Having been colonized by the European powers for several centuries, they produced large amounts of sugar that was sold around the globe at very high prices. In addition, albeit on a smaller scale, they produced other very profitable crops like indigo and coffee. Several of these islands were colonies of Great Britain, represented about one-third of the country's foreign trade. Thanks to direct taxes and duties from the Caribbean colonies, Britain was able to become the most important of the colonial powers during the eighteenth century. It was thus absolutely vital for the country to protect such a lucrative part of the ever-expanding British Empire. This became particularly true when, with the outbreak of the Revolutionary Wars, the British West Indies started to be menaced by the French (who had their own flourishing colonies in the Caribbean). Operating in the West Indies, however, was an immensely difficult undertaking for the British Army: the local tropical climate was wholly unbearable for European troops, who were frequently decimated by terrible local diseases such as the infamous tropical fevers. British soldiers understandably preferred avoiding service in the West Indies due to the unhealthy local conditions. To solve this problem and to garrison the nation's possessions in that part of the world, the British Army had no choice but to raise an increasing number of military units from the local communities of freed blacks. These were accustomed to the climate and temperatures of the Caribbean, and thus could physically cope with service in the theatre of operations. Until 1795, the British garrison of the West Indies was mostly made up of white regular regiments, which were sent in the Caribbean for periods of service before being transferred to other areas of the Empire. In that year, however, the British authorities finally decided to raise some regular West India Regiments from the free blacks living in their Caribbean colonies. The first eight such units were thus created, which had white officers and NCOs. These new regiments proved to be excellent corps, being employed successfully against the French and in putting down slave uprisings. As a result, in 1798 another four West India Regiments were recruited. During the Napoleonic Wars and afterwards, the number of regiments was drastically reduced, the British colonies in the Caribbean no longer being exposed to foreign attacks. By 1854, the British Army retained only three West India Regiments out of the original eight.

In the middle of the Atlantic Ocean, Britain controlled the small island of Saint Helena, where Napoleon had spent his final years in exile from 1815–21. Since 1842, the island had been garrisoned by Her Majesty's Saint Helena Regiment. This was a small line infantry unit consisting of just five companies, tasked with guarding Saint Helena as a strategic link located between Britain's various colonial possessions in the Atlantic. The corps was mostly composed of volunteers from other infantry regiments who were experienced soldiers of good conduct. Around 1850, the British had just a few colonial possessions of modest dimensions in Africa: these were located on the Gulf of Guinea in West Africa and consisted of small footholds extending along the coast. British possessions included portions of present-day Gambia, Ghana (at that time known as the Gold Coast) and Sierra Leone, where the British had their main base of Freetown. From the early 1850s, the regular British garrison of West Africa consisted of just three independent infantry companies that were collectively known as the Gold Coast Corps, which were tasked with performing police duties and were recruited from local black recruits who had white officers and NCOs. The Gold Coast Corps was usually supplemented by three companies taken from the West India Regiments (one from each of the existing units) that were detached for service in West Africa; each of these was garrisoned in one of the British settlements (Gambia, Gold Coast and Sierra Leone).

In 1806, the British expanded their colonial possessions in Africa by capturing the Cape of Good Hope (South Africa) from the Dutch. This was located in an important strategic position, controlling the commercial and naval routes connecting the Atlantic Ocean with the Pacific. For this reason, it had to be well garrisoned. The Dutch East India Company had established a permanent military garrison at the Cape of Good Hope since the late eighteenth century, consisting of locally recruited Hottentots and known as the Pandour Corps. In 1795, the British occupied the Cape of Good Hope for the first time and during the following year they reorganized the Pandour Corps as the new 300-strong Hottentot Corps. This was expanded in 1801 to become a regiment with ten companies, and was designated the Cape Regiment. Following the Peace of Amiens in 1802, the Cape of Good Hope was returned to the Dutch, who maintained the Cape Regiment but twice changed its denomination during the following years (first renaming it as the Corps of Free Hottentots and then the Hottentot Light Infantry). In 1806, the British seized the Cape of Good Hope permanently and reorganized the Cape Regiment once again. This now had ten companies, whose officers and NCOs were all whites, while the rankers were recruited from the Hottentots. These native troops were considered perfect light infantrymen, since they were used to living and fighting in the bush of South Africa. The original unit was expanded in 1817 with the addition of a light cavalry troop. In 1827, the cavalry component of the corps was disbanded and the number of infantry companies was reduced to three; these were soon transformed into companies of mounted riflemen who were armed with rifled carbines and wore dark green uniforms. Following these changes, the Cape Regiment was renamed once more as the Cape Mounted Rifles. Over time, most of the corps' NCOs were Hottentots and the unit showed great valour and a high level of mobility in fighting against hostile tribes menacing South Africa. By 1854, the Cape Mounted Rifles had been gradually expanded to comprise a total of twelve companies.

In 1796, the British captured the Dutch colony of Ceylon (modern Sri Lanka), a large island located just south of India; this was placed under the direct administration of the British Crown and thus was not part of the East India Company's possessions. The independent companies of Malays that had previously formed the garrison of Ceylon under the Dutch were consolidated by the British into a larger unit, known as the 1st Ceylon Regiment since 1801. During the following year, another regiment of this kind was organized for service in Ceylon, with a 3rd Ceylon Regiment created in 1805 and a 4th Regiment in 1810. The first unit established by the British on Ceylon was the best of all, consisting of nine line companies and one rifle company. By 1821, all the regiments organized by the British in Ceylon had been disbanded following the end of hostilities with Napoleonic France; only the 1st Ceylon Regiment was kept in service, having been transformed into a rifle corps in 1820. With the new denomination of the Ceylon Rifle Regiment, it made up the garrison of the island and was dressed in dark green. By 1854, it consisted of fourteen companies and it was a true multinational unit, since it comprised ten companies recruited from Malays as well as two from Indians and a further two from free blacks from East Africa.

Despite being located in Europe, Malta was administered as a colony by Britain, who garrisoned the Mediterranean island with a line infantry unit known as the Royal Malta Fencible Regiment. During the Napoleonic Wars, the British Army had included several units defined as 'fencible' or 'defencible'; these were garrison corps tasked with protecting a specific location, which were not deployed outside their home territories and were static in nature. The Royal Malta Fencible Regiment was formed in 1815 by Count Rivarola to act as the garrison of Malta. Despite its denomination, it consisted of a single battalion with ten companies. Seven of its companies acted as regular line infantry, while the remaining three consisted of artillerymen performing coastal defence. By 1854, the number of companies was reduced to six (three of infantry and three of artillery).

East India Company military units

The British presence in India became significant after the Battle of Plassey in 1757. Prior to that, other European colonial powers such as France and Portugal had been exerting a greater influence over India. From the time of its first territorial acquisitions in the Indian subcontinent, the British government had not annexed any Indian territory as a direct possession of the Crown; from a formal and practical point of view, British territories in India were all under the control of the East India Company. Established in 1600, the East India Company was a joint-stock company whose original main objective was to trade with the rich countries of the Asian continent. Like its Dutch equivalent operating in Indonesia, the British East India Company gradually emerged as a regional power in Asia and expanded its commercial influence by using political and military measures. The British traders eventually started to occupy important cities of India as well as tracts of coastline. All these new territories acted as outposts for the economic activities of the Company and were also the bases from where the British could exert their influence over the local Indian rulers. By the middle of the eighteenth century, with the decline of the great Moghul Empire, India was fractioned into a multitude of independent princedoms. These had outdated armies using traditional Indian weaponry and tactics, which were no match for the modern military technologies employed by the British. The East India Company was thus gradually able to use its powerful resources to transform several of the Indian native states into protectorates. Thanks to the signing of favourable trading treaties, the British acquired direct control over an increasing number of cities and territories. After Robert Clive's great victory at Plassey, with which the

French were almost expelled from India, the British process of expansion continued, with more possessions in the interior of the subcontinent.

During the following decades, the East India Company was forced to reorganize its military forces. The main task of these initially very small units was to protect the commercial interests of the Company and garrison its territorial possessions. From their foundation, the forces of the Company included a number of native soldiers, who were recruited with the help of local rulers who were allies of the Company, establishing a private military organization that was not part of the British Army. On many occasions, the European and native components of the East India Company's forces cooperated very well and efficiently in battle. With the reorganization that followed Plassey, their numbers were greatly increased and their standards of service became comparable to those of contemporary European armies. The native soldiers of the Company – known as sepoys – were Hindus or Muslims. Around the middle of the nineteenth century, the territorial possessions of the British East India Company were organized into three autonomous presidencies: Madras, Bengal and Bombay. Each of these presidencies had their own army, comprising both European units, largely made up of soldiers from Britain, and native corps recruited among the local Indian population but having British officers. Generally speaking, the European soldiers recruited by the Company in Britain were not of the same quality as those who served in the regular British Army, which offered better conditions of service to recruits and thus attracted the best elements wishing to serve in the military. Most of the British soldiers serving under the Company were individuals who had decided to leave their homeland in search of an opportunity or who had lived at the margins of society. Some of them had experienced problems with justice while others had no choice but to enlist as soldiers of fortune in order to earn a living. The Company's European units also included significant numbers of whites recruited in India from the many European adventurers or mercenaries who had voyaged there in search of employment. French, Swiss, German and Dutch recruits were the most common of these, but there were also individuals of mixed ethnicity (half-European and half-Indian). Discipline and training of these soldiers were not the same as for those serving in the British Army, but on most occasions these men proved reliable fighters. A good number of them had a clear idea of what military discipline was, since it was not uncommon for a soldier from the regular army to decide to remain in India after a period of service there and to sign up with the forces of the East India Company. Life in India was cheaper for them than in Britain, and the risks faced while serving under the flags of the Company were less than those experienced by soldiers in the regular army. From 1853, the European infantry of the East India Company consisted of nine regiments, with three for each presidency. It is important to note, however, that these units (despite their denomination) had the numerical consistency of a regular battalion, and that the companies comprising them usually served as independent detached units. The nine Company regiments consisted of the following:

Royal Madras Fusiliers
Madras Light Infantry
Madras Infantry
Royal Bengal Fusiliers
Bengal Fusiliers
Bengal Infantry
Royal Bombay Fusiliers
Bombay Light Infantry
Bombay Infantry

Some units were defined as light infantry, but in practice all had more or less the same characteristics. In 1862, following the Indian Mutiny, all the Company units were absorbed into the British Army as regular infantry.

The units of native infantry could trace their origins back to the early irregular bands of mercenaries that were established by the Company in India during the first decades of colonization. After Plassey, these irregular corps were gradually transformed into regular military units, their members receiving the denomination of sepoys. They started to wear uniforms of European cut and received modern firearms as well as proper training. Transforming the Indian mercenaries from irregular fighters into disciplined fusiliers was not a simple task, but the Indian recruits reached excellent standards of service. In Bengal, most of the sepoys were Hindus of high caste, who came in great numbers from the provinces bordering with Bengal. By the outbreak of the Crimean War, these were organized into seventy-four native battalions, each of which (like the European units) had the same establishment as their regular British equivalents. In Madras and Bombay, the sepoys did not come only from high castes, but included large numbers of Muslims. Generally speaking, all the native soldiers serving with the East India Company came from the so-called 'martial races': these were ethnic groups characterized by specific cultural features, traditionally linked with the profession of soldiery. In Madras there were fifty-two battalions of native infantry, while Bombay had only twenty-six. In total, the Company had 152 Indian battalions by the middle of the nineteenth century. In Bengal, the regular native infantry was supplemented by semi-regular corps of various types. Among these were the local infantry, consisting of battalions that were recruited in frontier areas in order to patrol the local border, with Indian junior officers (unlike the other sepoy units, whose officers were all whites). Around 1850, there were some fifty of these semi-regular units in Bengal. The Bengal Presidency could also deploy another category of troops, known as contingent forces, who had a lot in common with the local infantry and were also characterized by a semi-regular status. However, these were organized and paid by the various Indian princedoms that were allies of the East India Company. Following the First Sikh War, which ended in 1846, the military forces of Bengal were augmented by the creation of a new Frontier Force comprising four infantry regiments (mostly recruited from former soldiers of the Sikh Army). In 1851, these units, together with a new one of infantry and cavalry guides, were collectively renamed as the Punjab Irregular Force. This formation had as its main task the patrolling of the Punjab frontier and had a special status among the units of local infantry.

Generally speaking, the armies of the three presidencies were mostly made up of infantry units, having only a limited number of cavalry. The few horsemen they did have, however, could be of good quality, despite usually having a semi-regular status. In Bengal, the regular cavalry of the East India Company consisted entirely of native units, with ten regiments all designated as light cavalry (one of which was equipped with lances). In addition there was the Governor General's Bodyguard (formed of picked officers and men from the ordinary regiments) and eighteen regiments of irregular native cavalry. The latter were recruited by using the 'sillidar' system, under which local horsemen were to provide and maintain their own mounts and equipment. After the end of the Sikh War, another six cavalry units were recruited by the Company in Bengal: the guides already mentioned and five regiments collectively known as the Punjab Cavalry. In Madras, the regular cavalry consisted of eight light cavalry regiments made up of native soldiers, augmented by five regiments of horse provided by the Hyderabad princedom that were partly regularized and were later absorbed into the mounted forces of the Madras Presidency. In Bombay, the regular cavalry comprised three light cavalry regiments made up of native soldiers, the first of which was a lancer unit. These regulars were supplemented by four irregular corps: the Guzerat Irregular Horse, Scinde Irregular Horse, Poona Irregular Horse and South Mahratta Horse. The armies of the three presidencies also included some units of artillery and engineers, whose members were mostly Europeans and had an excellent reputation (being considered of practically the same level as their British Army equivalents). Bengal had three brigades of horse artillery (each with three European troops and one native troop), five battalions of European foot artillery (each with five companies) and two battalions of native foot artillery (each with two companies). Madras had one brigade of horse artillery (with four European troops and two native troops), three battalions of European foot artillery (each with four companies) and one battalion of native foot artillery (with six companies). Bombay had one brigade of horse artillery (with four European troops), two battalions of European foot artillery (each with four companies) and one battalion of native foot artillery (with ten companies). Each of the three presidencies had its own Engineer Corps, consisting of a small number of British officers with specific technical competencies. These officers were at the head of labour forces consisting of sappers, who were recruited from the local Indian communities. Bengal had six sapper companies, while Bombay had five and Madras just two.

Foreign military units

At the beginning of the Crimean War, the British Army experienced a serious shortage of manpower, being much smaller than its Russian opponent as well as its French ally. After the end of the Napoleonic Wars, Britain had greatly reduced its military forces for economic reasons. The British Army had been restructured to mostly perform policing and garrison duties across the many colonies that it had to protect. Britain was not ready for a full-scale conflict against a major military power on the European continent. Consequently, and with British soldiers being not particularly happy about serving for a long time in an inhospitable and faraway region like Crimea, the British authorities had no choice but to start recruiting units of foreign mercenaries in order to sustain the war effort. Something similar had happened during the Napoleonic Wars, and the British could also see the positive example of the French, who had formed their famous and effective Foreign Legion several years beforehand. The new foreign units were recruited from areas of Europe where potential soldiers of fortune were available in great numbers: Switzerland, Germany and Italy. These regions were all fragmented into small political entities that were completely autonomous but quite weak militarily, thus being perfect to provide volunteers for a foreign power like Britain. During the Napoleonic Wars, the British Army had recruited several excellent infantry units from the Swiss cantons, which had a long-established reputation as a homeland of mercenaries. Most of the European armies of the eighteenth and early nineteenth centuries included sizeable contingents of Swiss professional soldiers, so the British were confident that they could raise a large Swiss Legion and deploy it – very soon – in Crimea. The original plan was to form the following Swiss units: eight battalions of light infantry, two battalions of rifles, two regiments of cavalry and some elements of artillery/engineers. During the previous years, however, the political situation of Switzerland had changed dramatically following the civil war of 1847 that had seen two alliances of cantons fighting against each other. From 1852, the country had adopted a more centralized form of government, with the previous cantonal military contingents replaced by a unified Swiss Army. The new Helvetic government, soon after its creation, tried to limit as much as possible the foreign recruitment of mercenaries in Switzerland, so the British encountered serious difficulties in finding enough men. Nevertheless, the formation of Britain's Swiss Legion began in March 1854, when a recruiting committee and receiving depot were established by the British near Strasbourg (not far from the Swiss border). By the end of 1855, however, only two regiments of light infantry – with two battalions each – had been raised from Swiss volunteers. The 1st Regiment and the 1st Battalion of the 2nd Regiment were sent to Smyrna during early 1856, but the Crimean War ended before they could be sent into battle against the Russians. In May 1856, both regiments of the Swiss Legion were disbanded without having seen action and their men were repatriated.

During the Napoleonic Wars, the British Army had raised its best foreign units from Germany, in particular from the state of Hanover, which had been in personal union with Britain until the ascendancy of Queen Victoria in 1837. When the Crimean War began, the British authorities soon elaborated plans for the formation of a new German Legion, to be organized similarly to the famous King's German Legion that had fought with such success in the Napoleonic Wars. The German Prince Albert, consort of Queen Victoria, was enthusiastic about the idea of recruiting a legion from the German princedoms, striving to ensure the success of the project. In November 1854, Britain's Parliament passed the Foreign Enlistment Act, according to which foreigners could be enlisted in the British Army for the duration of the conflict with Russia and for service outside the British Isles. The German recruiting operation ran more smoothly than that for the Swiss, being organized by the commander of the German Legion, Major-General Richard von Stutterheim. He hired 200 recruiting agents in Germany and sent them to the major port cities, where large numbers of potential volunteers were available. The recruiters usually went to taverns and bought beer for young adventurers who might be interested in joining the ranks of the legion. By September 1855, Stutterheim, despite encountering strong opposition from the governments of the German princedoms, had been able to organize the following units: six regiments of light infantry with two battalions each, two regiments of rifles with two battalions each and one regiment of cavalry (light dragoons). These were sent to training camps in Britain, where they underwent a period of formation. Meanwhile, another regiment of rifles was in the process of being formed in Germany. Before the Crimean War ended, however, only the German Legion's 1st, 2nd and 3rd Regiments of Light Infantry and 1st Regiment of Rifles were dispatched in time to reach the theatre of operations. None of these saw action, but all of them

Uniforms of the Swiss Legion in British service. The officer on the left and the corporal on the right are from a light infantry unit, since they are dressed with the same M1855 uniform as the British line/light infantry. The officer in the centre is from one of the two rifle battalions, whose formation was never completed. He is dressed in dark green like the British Rifle Brigade. The Italian Legion in British service was dressed in red exactly like the British line/light infantry.

Uniforms of the German Legion in British service (from left to right): rifleman, light infantryman and officer of the light cavalry. The rifles were dressed in dark green like their British equivalents, the light infantry wore red like those of the Swiss Legion and Italian Legion, and the light cavalry (despite being designed as light dragoons) were uniformed like the British hussars.

suffered losses due to cholera. Upon the disbandment of their legion, the German mercenaries could choose to return home (at the expense of the British government) or move to Cape Colony, where they could settle down as soldier-colonists. Each German mercenary was to receive an acre of land but would have been tasked with defending the colony of South Africa from attacks by the local natives. Around 2,300 German soldiers arrived at the Cape in the early weeks of 1857; they settled down as military colonists, but never adapted to the living conditions of South Africa. In 1858, around 1,400 members of the German Legion – which had not yet been formally disbanded – were sent to India to help put down the Indian Mutiny. Once again, however, they arrived too late to play any role in the campaign. Six hundred of the Germans returned to South Africa, the others joining the ranks of the East India Company's European military units (which were soon absorbed into the British Army). The German Legion was officially disbanded in 1861, several of its members having joined the ranks of the Cape Mounted Rifles.

According to the original plans that were approved for the formation of the three foreign legions, the British would have recruited a total of 20,000 mercenaries: 10,000 Germans, 5,000 Swiss and 5,000 Italians. These numbers looked sufficiently large to avoid the introduction of conscription in Britain, something that most of the other European armies had to do in order to deploy sizeable military contingents. As we will see in a following chapter, Britain could count on the alliance of Piedmont in Italy; the Piedmontese, in fact, joined the anti-Russian international coalition in order to gain the diplomatic support of Britain and France. Piedmont was preparing for a war against the Austrian Empire and had ambitions of completing the unification of Italy. The only way for them to have hopes of winning a conflict against the Austrians was to obtain the support of Britain and France, hence the decision of the Piedmontese government to enter the Crimean War. The British, in addition to counting on the large expeditionary force sent by the Piedmontese, wanted to recruit an Italian Legion of mercenaries from the other Italian states. With the help of Piedmont but encountering the strong opposition of the Austrians, the British were able to recruit three regiments of light infantry and one regiment of rifles for their Italian Legion. These were trained in Piedmont but were not ready to fight until the hostilities with Russia were coming to an end. In 1856, with the Treaty of Paris about to be signed between the opposing powers, the Italian Legion had reached the island of Malta en route to Crimea. It was disbanded in the summer of the same year due to the indiscipline of many of its members (several of whom were former Lombard or Sicilian revolutionaries) without having seen action. As has been made clear, the plans for foreign legions of mercenaries organized for employment in the Crimean War were a total failure and gave no significant contribution to the British cause. Times had changed since the days of the Napoleonic Wars, the emergence of new nationalistic feelings across Europe having ruined the possibility of recruiting effective mercenary contingents.

In addition to recruiting soldiers of fortune from Europe, the British also tried to establish some auxiliary contingents by using Ottoman soldiers. The British first attempted to discipline the *bashi-bazouks*, the irregular soldiers of the Ottoman Army, in the hope of transforming them into something comparable to the Indian native cavalry serving under the East India Company. William Ferguson Beatson, a major serving in the forces of the East India Company later known as 'Shemshi Pasha', was tasked with forming a semi-disciplined corps of *bashi-bazouks* that was called Beatson's Horse or the Osmanli Irregular Cavalry. Beatson, together with several other capable British officers, recruited a total of 4,000 Ottoman irregulars who were assembled into a cavalry division: 1,000 Anatolians, 1,000 Syrians, 1,000 Albanians/Bosnians and 1,000 Macedonians. Paid by the British, these men were divided into five regiments that had small cadres of British officers. Beatson's Horse was ready to fight by the end of 1854, but Lord Raglan (overall commander of the British expeditionary force) was never fully convinced about their combat capabilities and thus never authorized their employment. After some episodes of indiscipline and a chronic lack of funds, Beatson's Horse was finally disbanded in September 1855. During the autumn of 1855, some of the best elements from the disbanded irregular cavalry were re-enlisted by the British to form the new Osmanli Irregular Cavalry, but they never had any proper organization and were disbanded in July 1856 without having seen much action.

Soon after their arrival in the Ottoman Empire, the British understood that the Turkish infantry had great potential as soldiers but needed competent officers/NCOs in order to perform well on the battlefield. It was therefore agreed with the Ottoman authorities to organize a large Anglo-Turkish Contingent, an infantry force consisting of Turkish soldiers trained and commanded by British officers and NCOs. The basic idea was to create a 'westernized' Ottoman contingent that would have been similar to the forces of the East India Company: some entire regiments of the Turkish line infantry would have transferred to British service after having been deprived of their incompetent native officers and NCOs. The Ottoman authorities were not particularly enthusiastic about the idea of ceding some of their best soldiers to the British, but in the end they had no choice but to accept the proposal. By August 1855, the Anglo-Turkish Contingent consisted of ten regiments of line infantry, two regiments of cavalry and four batteries of artillery. Of these units, seven regiments of line infantry, both units of cavalry and one battery of artillery came from the Redeef (Reserve) of the Ottoman Army and not from Turkish regular forces. After a few months, the Anglo-Turkish Contingent received its definitive organization; it was now to consist of sixteen regiments of line infantry assembled into four brigades with four regiments each, three regiments of cavalry, six batteries of foot artillery, one battery of horse artillery, a battery of garrison artillery, an engineer corps (including a small 'telegraph detachment') and a transport corps. Most of the officers who commanded

British officer of the corps known as Beatson's Horse, a unit made up of semi-regularized *bashi-bazouks*. The British officers of this unit wore the simple uniform shown here, consisting of an emerald green *kurtka* or blouse that was very similar to the one used by the contemporary native cavalry of the East India Company.

these various units came from the armies of the East India Company and had enlisted into the Anglo-Turkish Contingent to obtain 'easy' promotions while serving in the Ottoman Army: lieutenant-colonels became colonels, majors became lieutenant-colonels, captains became majors and lieutenants became captains. The new brevets

Bashi-bazouk from Beatson's Horse dressed in his usual civilian clothes, like all the irregulars of the Ottoman Army. The soldiers of the Anglo-Turkish Contingent were dressed like the line infantrymen of the Ottoman Army, but had the cuffs of their tunics in the distinctive colours that the British instructors assigned to each of the Anglo-Turkish Contingent's sixteen regiments. The British officers and NCOs of the corps wore dark blue or red peaked caps with a brass crescent on the front and dark blue shell jackets. The jackets had the badge of the Anglo-Turkish Contingent (featuring the monogram of Queen Victoria) embroidered on the right sleeve above the pointed cuff.

received by these officers obviously corresponded to higher pay, which was provided by the British authorities. The 17,000 men of the Anglo-Turkish Contingent mostly performed auxiliary duties during the closing months of the Crimean War, including garrisoning important locations, before being disbanded in May 1856. In addition

Arab *bashi-bazouk* in Ottoman service. This was the appearance of the short-lived Spahis d'Orient recruited by the French for the Crimean War. The profusion of old-fashioned weapons was typical of the Ottoman irregular soldiers.

The British Army 71

Contemporary print showing a British officer of the Osmanli Horse Artillery. The uniform is similar to that of the Horse Artillery Brigade: red 'Albert' helmet with red horsehair mane, dark blue hussar jacket with golden frontal frogging and dark blue trousers with golden side-stripes. The golden 'Hungarian knots' embroidered on the sleeves showed an officer's rank.

to the Anglo-Turkish Contingent, the British raised another independent regular corps from Turkish soldiers: the Osmanli Horse Artillery, consisting of four troops of mounted artillery (equipped with 9-pdr guns and 24-pdr howitzers), commanded by twelve British officers (most of whom were former NCOs). Created by William Beatson, this corps was intended to be part of Beatson's Horse, but after the latter was disbanded it was attached to the Anglo-Turkish Contingent.

Chapter 2

The French Army

The French Army of 1854 was considered by many contemporary observers to be the best military force of Europe, having been completely reformed and reorganized by Napoleon III during the previous year. After the end of the Napoleonic Wars, France had soon restored its status as a great power and had endured some chaotic years politically. Between 1815 and 1830, the country had been ruled by the restored Bourbon monarchy and had begun to have a growing colonial interest, culminating in the invasion of Algeria in 1830. In the same year, a popular revolution at home had obliged the monarchy to adopt a constitution, and a new king – Louis Philippe – had been placed on the throne. Louis Philippe, known as the 'citizen king' because of his support for the ascending middle classes, worked hard to modernize the French Army and enlarge the country's political sphere of influence. Paris was ravaged by a new popular revolution in 1848, which caused the definitive end of the French monarchy, and France became a republic for the second time since the revolution of the late eighteenth century. New democratic institutions were created and elections took place; these were won by Louis Napoleon Bonaparte, son of Louis Bonaparte (Napoleon I's younger brother and former King of Holland until 1810). Bonapartism had always remained strong in France, even after the restoration of the Bourbons in 1815. Indeed, many Frenchmen looked back at the years of the Napoleonic Wars with great nostalgia. Napoleon I had made them great by dominating the battlefields of Europe, and they never renounced their dreams of regaining that greatness. Louis Napoleon Bonaparte, backed by strong popular support, was soon able to obtain complete control over the French state by destroying any form of internal opposition. In 1851, after three years of presidency, he mounted a military coup and gained absolute powers, then in December 1852 he officially restored the Napoleonic Empire and transformed France back into a monarchy. France's Second Empire had been born, and the new monarch took the name of Napoleon III (to show his personal respect for Napoleon II, the young son of the original Napoleon, who had died at a very young age). The Second Empire had a religious cult for the First Empire: all the political and military institutions created by Napoleon I were copied and restored in an attempt to show to the world that the glory of France had returned. The units of the French Army were given Imperial

Eagles that were almost identical to those carried in the Napoleonic Wars, and also received new uniforms – unrivalled for their elegance – that were of clear Napoleonic cut. Their participation in the Crimean War was the first major test for the forces of the Second Empire, which showed great valour in clashes against the Russians, initiating a new period of French victories that would only end with humiliating defeat by Prussia in 1870.

Imperial Guard

During the reign of Napoleon I, the most feared corps of the French Army had been the Imperial Guard, a miniature army that comprised many different units from each branch of service. The Imperial Guard was formed by the best soldiers of the French Empire and was tasked with protecting the emperor and performing special duties on the battlefield. It was an elite corps, whose members enjoyed a series of privileges such as higher pay and better conditions of service. Napoleon III, following the example of his more famous predecessor, reorganized the Imperial Guard soon after the Second Empire was proclaimed. It would be a mistake, however, to think that the new Imperial Guard was just an updated version of the original one. First of all, Napoleon III's Imperial Guard had a new primary function: protecting the absolutistic regime created by the new monarch from internal threats. This was something that the original Imperial Guard had done only on a limited scale, since Napoleon I never faced a particularly strong internal opposition. Secondly, the new Imperial Guard consisted entirely of French units, whereas the original one had comprised several units made up of foreigners. This was due to the fact that Napoleon I had created his Imperial Guard after conquering the Empire, while Napoleon III had formed his new version of the formation in the hope of forging an empire. Finally, it should be noted that some units from the original Imperial Guard were not re-formed, but were replaced by new ones that did not exist during the Napoleonic Wars.

Napoleon III's Imperial Guard was officially created on 1 May 1854. According to the Imperial Decree that detailed its formation, it was to consist of the following units: two regiments of grenadiers, two regiments of voltigeurs, one battalion of chasseurs, one regiment of cuirassiers, one regiment of guides, one regiment of gendarmerie, one regiment of mounted artillery and one company of engineers. The grenadiers were the heavy infantry component of the Imperial Guard; their two regiments had three battalions each (increased to four in January 1855). The voltigeurs were light infantrymen, the heirs of Napoleon I's foot chasseurs, and their two regiments also had three battalions each (increased to four in January

1855). The single battalion of chasseurs was a light infantry unit equipped with rifled carbines, which did not exist in the original Imperial Guard. The cuirassiers were heavy cavalrymen equipped with metal helmets and cuirasses, the heirs in the history of the Guard of Napoleon I's horse grenadiers. The guides were created by converting an existing regiment of mounted chasseurs (light cavalry) and retained all their main features. As the mounted chasseurs of the Imperial Guard had been Napoleon I's favourite unit, Napoleon III decided to reform them with the new denomination of 'Guides' in order to show some degree of autonomy from his predecessor. Both the cuirassiers and the guides had four squadrons each. The regiment of gendarmerie was a foot unit, tasked with performing military police duties; it was expanded in August 1854 with the addition of a single mounted squadron. The mounted artillery had six companies/batteries of horse-drawn light guns. On 17 February 1855, various new units were added to the Imperial Guard: one regiment of Zouaves (colonial light infantry, which will be covered in the section on the Army of Africa), one regiment of foot artillery (with eight

French infantry of the Imperial Guard (from left to right): voltigeur, grenadier, drummer of the grenadiers and drum-major of the grenadiers. Yellow was the distinctive colour of the voltigeurs since the Napoleonic era. Note the additional decorative elements worn by the drum-major (such as the coloured plume).

French foot units of the Imperial Guard (from left to right): Zouave, chasseur, foot artilleryman and foot gendarme. Note the use of the brown *jambiéres* worn over the white spats and the black bearskin worn by both the foot artillery and foot gendarmerie.

companies/batteries of field guns) and one squadron of the train (tasked with transporting the guns of the foot artillery).

In December 1855, due to France's heavy involvement in the Crimean War, Napoleon III decided to significantly expand his Imperial Guard by forming several new regiments: one of grenadiers, two of voltigeurs, one of cuirassiers, one of dragoons, one of mounted chasseurs and one of lancers. In order to form the new infantry regiments, the existing units of grenadiers and voltigeurs reduced the internal establishment of their battalions from eight to six companies. The 3rd Grenadiers, 3rd Voltigeurs and 4th Voltigeurs had four battalions each, three of which were formed from veteran soldiers who were already fighting in Crimea, while the remaining battalion was recruited in France. The 2nd Cuirassiers (with four squadrons) was also created from veterans fighting in Crimea, while the 1st Cuirassiers had been recruited from the best elements of the French Army's heavy cavalry regiments. The dragoons, known as the Empress' Dragoons like those of Napoleon I, also consisted of four squadrons made up of chosen veterans. The mounted chasseurs, with four squadrons – formed under strong pressure from the French public to have one such

Uniforms of the French Zouaves of the Imperial Guard. The turban, trimmed jacket and loose trousers were all clearly inspired by Algerian native dress. The drum-major and sapper on the right are easily recognizable: the former has additional golden embroidering on the jacket and waistcoat, while the latter has a specific badge embroidered on the sleeves and gauntlet gloves.

unit to preserve the heritage of Napoleon I's Imperial Guard – mostly consisted of Crimean veterans from the disbanded 4th Regiment of African Chasseurs (see the section below on the Army of Africa for more details). The four squadrons of lancers were made up of the best elements from the line units of dragoons and lancers. A second company of engineers was also created in December 1855. Despite being intended as a reserve force to be used only in an emergency, the Imperial Guard sent several of its units to fight in the Crimean War, and these all performed extremely well. This was in consequence of all the line regiments of the French Army being obliged to nominate their most experienced soldiers of good character for service in the Imperial Guard.

In addition to the Imperial Guard, Napoleon III also created another small elite corps that performed ceremonial duties despite not being part of the Guard: the Cent-gardes Squadron (Hundred Guardsmen Squadron). This unit was formed on 25 March 1854, before the Imperial Guard, and constituted the mounted bodyguard of the emperor. Its members were chosen for their loyalty towards the new regime

French trooper of the Cent-gardes Squadron. The uniform is extremely elegant, with a profusion of golden elements.

The French Army

French cuirassier (left) and mounted gendarme (right) of the Imperial Guard.

and were all extremely tall; they were equipped as heavy cavalry with metal helmets and cuirasses. Napoleon I had never had a similar ceremonial military corps, which had a lot in common with the small units that made up the French Royal Household until 1830. During his turbulent life, the future Napoleon III had spent several years as a political exile in Britain, where he had admired the magnificent horsemen of the Household Cavalry. By forming the Cent-gardes, he wanted to create something similar to the British Horse Guards, who had been given cuirasses soon after the end of the Napoleonic Wars. The 100 soldiers of the Cent-gardes Squadron were tasked with protecting their monarch and garrisoning the Imperial palace. They had the privilege of wearing the most elegant uniform of the French Army and were chosen from among the best soldiers of the line cavalry. They created a real spectacle when riding through the streets of Paris. They received higher pay and had better living conditions than members of the Imperial Guard, but did not participate in the conflict with Russia.

French lancer of the Imperial Guard. The curious white uniform, a colour rarely used by the French Army, is in clear Polish style.

French troopers of the guides (left) and mounted artillery (right) of the Imperial Guard. Both uniforms are in obvious hussar style.

Infantry

In 1815, after Napoleon's crushing defeat at the Battle of Waterloo, the French Army had to be rebuilt almost from scratch. The newly restored Bourbons wanted to eliminate all the remaining Bonapartists from the ranks of the military, and under pressure from their former enemies to adopt a less aggressive political attitude they restructured the French Army on Departmental Legions, disbanding the previous regiments that had been strongly linked with Napoleon. The Departmental Legions were small territorial armies, comprising units from the various branches of service. Each department of France had one of these legions (for a total of eighty-six), each of which consisted of the following: two battalions of line infantry, one battalion of light infantry, one troop of light cavalry and one company of light artillery. This structure, introduced in 1818, was soon abandoned when France regained its previous military status. The French infantry was reorganized in 1820 on sixty line and twenty light regiments. The departmental recruiting system was abandoned, and each of the new regiments comprised two battalions, except for the first forty of line infantry that had three battalions each. Each line battalion had eight companies: six of fusiliers, one of grenadiers (heavy infantry) and one of voltigeurs (light infantry). A single light battalion had six companies of chasseurs, one of carabiniers (heavy infantry) and one of voltigeurs (light infantry). The voltigeurs were not true light infantry, being skirmishers who operated in open order in front of the advancing battalions. Their skirmish line delivered a speedy rather than accurate fire. They were armed with smoothbore carbines, which were easier to reload than rifled muskets but were not very accurate. In 1824, the line infantry was expanded to sixty-four regiments, each of three battalions.

During this period, as had been the case during the Napoleonic Wars, there was very little difference between the line and light units of the French infantry. The light regiments were uniformed and equipped almost identically to the line ones, no special light infantry training existed and no units of rifles were created. The line infantry was expanded to sixty-six regiments in 1830, each now with four battalions, and a third battalion was added to every light infantry regiment. One battalion of each foot regiment was a depot one. In 1821, the number of light infantry units was increased to twenty-one. The new Delvigne carbine, a rifled weapon for the light infantry, started to be tested by the French Army in 1833, and some years later the Duke of Orleans, the son of Louis Philippe, was authorized to create an experimental company of riflemen equipped with this carbine. Tests conducted by the new chasseurs à pied (foot chasseurs) had very positive results, following which a new kind of light infantry was born in the French Army, equipped with rifled weapons and undergoing specific training. The new riflemen were excellent marksmen, wore less extravagant uniforms (they did not have the red trousers of the line infantry) and had black belt equipment instead of the more visible and usual white. In April 1838, the experimental corps was transformed into a battalion with six companies, then in 1840, following excellent performance in combat in Algeria, the chasseurs à pied were expanded and structured on ten independent battalions, each of eight companies. In 1840, the regular light infantry was expanded with the raising of another four regiments.

In 1841, the line infantry was increased to seventy-five regiments with three battalions each, and the number of companies in each battalion was reduced to seven (one of heavy infantry, one of light infantry, four of fusiliers or chasseurs and one depot). In case of war mobilization, a fourth battalion was to be added to each regiment and the number of companies in each battalion was to be increased to nine. In 1848, all the foot battalions were restructured on eight companies: one of heavy infantry, one of light infantry and six of fusiliers or chasseurs. After Napoleon III became emperor in 1852, the internal establishment of the foot regiments was changed again, with each of them consisting of two active battalions of eight companies and one reserve battalion with seven companies.

Uniforms of the French infantry (from left to right): line infantryman, officer of the line infantry, chasseur (light infantryman) and Zouave. As prescribed by the 1852 dress regulations that were respected by the whole French Army, the line infantry had red facings and trousers while the light infantry had green facings and light blue trousers.

In 1853, another ten battalions of riflemen were formed. Napoleon III was not happy with his traditional light infantry, realizing that the light troops of the future would have to be equipped with rifled weapons. As a result, on 24 October 1854, he decided to transform the twenty-five regiments of light infantry into regiments of line infantry. With the inclusion of the former light infantry units – that were numbered 76–100 – the French line infantry now comprised a total of 100 regiments. The light infantry, after these changes, consisted only of chasseurs à pied battalions. In 1855, their number was increased from twenty to twenty-two, but the two new units were short-lived, being disbanded in 1856. Due to the mobilization for the Crimean War, the line infantry was also expanded, with the creation of two new regiments; these too were disbanded in 1856. According to the new structure introduced in 1855, each line regiment was to consist of three active battalions and one depot battalion. An active battalion had one company of grenadiers, one company of voltigeurs and four companies of fusiliers. The depot battalions each had six companies of fusiliers.

Cavalry

Several years after the end of its glorious era in the Napoleonic Wars, the French cavalry was completely reorganized in 1825. It thereafter consisted of three main categories: reserve cavalry, line cavalry and light cavalry. The reserve cavalry was the heavy branch, with regiments equipped with metal cuirasses. It was a shock force tasked with making battlefield charges, and comprised both carabiniers and cuirassiers. The line cavalry was the medium branch and consisted of regiments which could act as a shock force but also perform duties like scouting, comprising both dragoons and lancers. The light cavalry were highly mobile regiments tasked with scouting and skirmishing, and featured units of mounted chasseurs and hussars. Regiments of the reserve and line cavalry had five squadrons each (four active and one depot), while those of the light cavalry had six squadrons (five active and one depot). The carabiniers were the most aristocratic soldiers of the French cavalry, their officers coming from leading families of the French nobility with long military traditions. They had not been disbanded during the Revolution and had been kept in service by Napoleon I, who gave them metal helmets and cuirasses to improve their performance in combat. With the restoration

French carabineer (left) and cuirassier (right). The metal helmet and cuirass of the carabineers was covered with golden-coloured copper in order to create a distinctive appearance.

The French Army 85

French officers of the mounted chasseurs (left) and the dragoons (right).

French lancer wearing full dress.

The French Army 87

French mounted chasseur.

French officer of the hussars.

French hussar.

of the Bourbons in 1815, the 1st Carabiniers had been transformed into a heavy cavalry unit tasked with escorting the brother of the king, but the 2nd Carabiniers was disbanded. However, the 2nd Carabiniers was re-raised in 1825, using the best elements of the existing cuirassier regiments. In 1830, the 1st Carabiniers received their old denomination and ceased to perform as a guard corps. As a result, there were two regiments of carabiniers in the French Army in 1854, and they were considered to be the elite of the heavy cavalry. The cuirassiers, meanwhile, consisted of ten regiments, the last four of which were established in 1825. The dragoons numbered twelve regiments, the last two of which were formed in 1825. With the restoration of 1815, the lancer units that had been part of the Napoleonic army were all disbanded, except for the Red Lancers of the Imperial Guard (the former Dutch Lancers), who were transformed into the new Lancers of the Royal Guard. In 1830, however, the latter became a line unit (the 1st Regiment of Lancers) and thus lost their guard status. Another five regiments of line lancers were created in 1831 by converting and re-equipping with lances the oldest five regiments of mounted chasseurs. Another two regiments of mounted chasseurs became lancers in 1836, meaning that by 1854, the French cavalry comprised a total of eight lancer units. By the outbreak of the Crimean War, the French Army had thirteen regiments of mounted chasseurs, all of which had been formed in 1815 and had been the mounted branch of the Departmental Legions organized from 1818. After the restoration of the Bourbons in 1815, there were six regiments of French hussars, their number being increased to nine in 1840 when three new units were formed.

Artillery and technical corps

Napoleon III, like his more famous predecessor, had a passion for artillery and a deep knowledge of all matters relating to the production and employment of field guns. In his youth he had even helped to design a new 12-pdr cannon, which was called 'Napoleon' in his honour and was widely employed during the American Civil War. By the time of the Crimean War, the French artillery was still equipped with smoothbore muzzle-loaders, rifled breech-loaders having not yet been introduced (being in the process of early testing). The artillery enjoyed a series of privileges in the French Army, mostly because its officers were well-educated men who had specific technical skills and had been promoted due to their personal capabilities. Meritocracy was sometimes neglected in the French military, but not in the artillery, which also enjoyed the privilege of having an autonomous general staff. On 14 February 1854, Napoleon III completely reorganized the French artillery to comprise the following branches: foot artillery or reserve artillery, line artillery, mounted artillery and pontonniers. The foot/reserve artillery, equipped with heavy 12-pdr guns and 16-pdr howitzers, was tasked with bombarding enemy fortifications during sieges and forming a general reserve during pitched battles. The line artillery, equipped with 12-pdr guns, was tasked with supporting the infantry with the fire of its field guns. The mounted artillery, equipped with light 8-pdr guns, had a high level of mobility thanks to its horse-drawn pieces. The pontonniers formed a

French gunner of the foot artillery (left) and corporal of the engineers (right).

92   Armies of the Crimean War, 1853–1856

French trooper of the mounted artillery.

pontoon corps attached to the artillery. In 1855, the general structure of the French artillery was as follows: five regiments of foot/reserve artillery, each with twelve field batteries and six siege batteries; seven regiments of line artillery with fifteen field batteries each; four regiments of mounted artillery, each with eight field batteries;

and one regiment of pontonniers with sixteen companies. Additionally, there were some various auxiliary corps: twelve companies of artillery workers, two companies of armourers and four companies of veteran artillerymen. The artillery had its own train, responsible for transporting the guns and their ammunition, organized on two regiments with sixteen companies each. The Engineer Corps of the French Army had its own autonomous staff, like the artillery, and comprised very competent officers who commanded a labour force of sappers. It was organized as three regiments with two battalions each; a single battalion comprised nine companies of sappers. There were also three independent reserve companies. In addition to the artillery train there was the Train des Equipages Militaires, whose task was to transport all the materials of the army that did not belong to the artillery. This consisted of three regiments with sixteen companies each, plus four independent companies.

Naval and colonial troops

As France lost most of its old royal overseas colonies during the Napoleonic Wars, between 1815 and 1830 it could no longer be considered a great colonial power. In 1830, however, the French invaded Algeria, a country that it took them several decades to fully occupy. The occupation of Algiers marked the beginning of a new phase in the history of French colonialism, which continued under the rule of Napoleon III, who, made the first important steps towards the colonization of what became French Indochina. From 1683, France's colonial possessions were garrisoned by a specific category of troops known as the Troupes de la Marine (Naval Troops), which was part of the French Navy, not the Army. Algeria was an exception to this rule, as this colony was considered part of metropolitan France and thus had its own autonomous garrison troops (known as the Army of Africa, which was formally part of the metropolitan military and will be covered in a separate section below). By 1854, in addition to Algeria, France controlled the following colonial possessions: the islands of Martinique and Guadeloupe in the Caribbean, Guiana in South America, the small island of Saint-Pierre-et-Miquelon in the northern Atlantic, Senegal in West Africa, the islands of Saint Marie and La Réunion in the Indian Ocean, the city of Pondicherry and some other coastal bases in south-eastern India, and Tahiti in the Pacific Ocean. All these colonies were manned by Naval Troops, which consisted of infantry as well as artillery. The Troupes de la Marine had a very peculiar status, since they acted both as naval troops (marines) and colonial troops. The original decision of assigning the defence of overseas territories to the Ministry of the Navy had been a very wise one for the French, producing very good results in the long run. In 1822, after the terrible defeats of the Napoleonic Wars,

French sergeant of the naval infantry.

the Naval Troops had been reorganized on two regiments of naval infantry and one regiment of naval artillery. In 1828, a third regiment of naval infantry was added. From 1838, each of the three naval infantry regiments had a large establishment with thirty companies, for a total of ninety that were distributed in the various colonies as follows: forty-five in France (deployed in the French Navy's main bases of Brest, Cherbourg, Rochefort and Toulon), fifteen in Guadeloupe, fifteen in Martinique, six in Guiana, three in Senegal and six in La Réunion. In 1843, the 1st Naval Infantry Regiment and 3rd Naval Infantry Regiment were expanded to forty-one companies, while the 2nd Naval Infantry Regiment was expanded to thirty-eight companies. By 1854, the 120 companies and 15,000 soldiers of the naval infantry were distributed as follows across the French colonies: seventy-nine companies in the naval bases of metropolitan France, eight in Martinique, eight in Guadeloupe, nine in Guiana, seven in Senegal, five in La Réunion and four in the Pacific Ocean. The single regiment of naval artillery organized in 1822 consisted of twenty-five companies distributed among the five most important ports of France, plus five companies of naval artillery workers. In 1840, the number of naval artillery companies was increased to forty, but just two years later they were reduced to thirty. The naval artillery was tasked with garrisoning the main bases of the French Navy, but also provided small detachments of naval artillerymen who served on the warships of the fleet as well as in the various colonies. In addition to the 120 companies of naval infantry and thirty companies of naval artillery, the Troupes de la Marine also comprised some locally recruited native colonial units in some of France's overseas possessions. Senegal had two infantry companies – which later became the famous Senegalese Tirailleurs – and one squadron of cavalry. The latter, which later became the Senegalese Spahis, initially consisted of a squadron detached from the 1st Regiment of Algerian Spahis (see the Army of Africa below). What remained of the once-glorious French possessions in India had a small corps of cipahis or sepoys, local soldiers which was organized on two companies of infantry that acted as gendarmerie.

The Army of Africa

Soon after the occupation of Algiers in 1830, the French faced two main problems. Firstly, they had to find a way to garrison the newly conquered territories without using the units that had made up the expeditionary corps, since most of these were due to return to France; and secondly, they had to demobilize the defeated forces of the Ottoman Regency of Algiers without causing a native uprising. There was one possible solution to these two problems: forming native auxiliary corps recruited from the former Ottoman soldiers, which could help the French in garrisoning Algiers. General Clauzel, who commanded the French forces in Algiers, realized this project by ordering – on 1 October 1830 – the creation of a first unit of native infantry. The members of this new corps soon became known as Zouaves, from the name of the Kabyle 'Zwawa' tribes from which they were recruited. The Zwawa communities, living in Algeria and Tunisia, had always provided excellent soldiers to the Ottomans, and thus had a well-established military tradition. The new Zouave Corps initially had just four companies, which were soon expanded to eight. Before the organization of the first unit could be completed, however, on 21 December 1830, Clauzel decided to expand the Zouaves to two battalions with eight companies each. The Zouaves experienced many difficulties in their early years, with desertion rates extremely high, and the French struggled to maintain the two battalions. In order to reach the planned establishments, an increasing number of French volunteers had to be admitted into the Zouaves' ranks. Initially only the officers and NCOs of the two battalions had been French, but by 1833 a third of the rankers were not Algerian. Many French soldiers who were part of the garrison left in Algiers volunteered to become Zouaves: discipline was not so strict in the corps and a ranker had more opportunities to become a corporal or sergeant. In addition, the French volunteers were greatly attracted by the magnificent uniforms of the Zouaves. Moorish in style, these consisted of an idealized version of the Zwawa communities' tribal dress that was heavily influenced by the Romantic aesthetic ideals of the time. In 1831, to complete the organization of the two battalions, the French authorities were obliged to recruit some inexperienced volunteers from Paris. These, organized into a volunteer corps known as the Volontaires Parisiens, were former revolutionaries who had fought against King Charles X in July 1830 and were sent to Algeria after the end of the revolution. On 7 March 1833, the Zouaves officially became a *corps mixte*, i.e. a military corps made up of local recruits and French volunteers. The two existing battalions were disbanded in order to form a single battalion of ten companies. Two of the companies were entirely made up of French volunteers, while the remaining eight each had sixty-two Algerian and twelve French soldiers. A 2nd Battalion of Zouaves was formed in 1835, followed two years later by a 3rd Battalion. However, the recruiting problems experienced during the previous years continued, the number of Algerians wishing to serve in the corps remaining very limited. The 3rd Battalion of Zouaves was disbanded due to the lack of recruits on 4 August 1839, but it was re-raised just eight months later. On 8 September 1841, the three existing battalions were assembled into a single regiment and received a more stable structure, the internal establishment of each battalion increased to eight active companies and one depot company.

Two months after the Zouaves' reorganization, a new force of tirailleurs (light infantry) was created, and since this unit consisted entirely of Algerians, the number of native soldiers in the Zouave regiment started to decrease very rapidly. Initially, the 8th Company of each battalion continued to be made up of local recruits, but by 1848 there were no more Algerians in the Zouave Regiment (which officially ceased to be a *corps mixte* in 1849). With the reorganization of 1841–42, the Zouaves had started to include a number of conscripts, but these remained quite limited since the flow of volunteers wishing to serve in their ranks remained significant. On 13 February 1852, Napoleon III ordered a general expansion of the Zouaves, which was restructured on three regiments with three battalions each. The existing three units became the first battalions of the three new regiments, and the internal organization of these battalions did not change. With the reform of 1852, the Zouaves also received light infantry status, having previously mostly acted as line infantry; for example, they replaced their drummers with trumpeters.

In April 1854, following the outbreak of the Crimean War, the Zouaves were called to serve outside North Africa for the first time in their history. Each of the three regiments was asked to provide two Bataillons de Marche (marching battalions), temporary units created to serve overseas for the duration of a conflict. The six temporary battalions, having eight companies each, were formed with the best elements from each regiment and were assembled together into three temporary regiments with two battalions each. The battalions of the 1st Regiment were assigned to the 1st Division of General Canrobert, those of the 2nd Regiment to the 3rd Division of General Bonaparte and those of the 3rd Regiment to the 2nd Division of General Bosquet. The Zouaves fought with incredible courage and great determination during the Crimean War, winning the admiration of Napoleon III as well as of their enemies. At the Battle of the Alma (20 September 1854), the battalions of the 3rd Regiment of Zouaves launched a surprise attack against the Russians after advancing on broken terrain, capturing enemy guns and using them against the Russians. Following this action, a magnificent statue representing a Zouave was placed under the newly renamed Alma Bridge in Paris and Napoleon III decided to raise a new Zouave regiment for his recently formed Imperial Guard. The Regiment of Zouaves of the Imperial Guard was officially established on 23 December 1854 and consisted of two battalions with seven companies each. The new corps was recruited in Crimea from the best elements of the Zouaves and of the metropolitan light infantry who were fighting against the Russians. Meanwhile, the Zouaves continued to distinguish themselves during operations, especially at the Battle of Balaclava (25 October 1854) and Battle of Inkerman (5 November 1854). Now including the Zouaves of the Imperial Guard, they also played a prominent role during the decisive Battle of Malakoff (7 September 1855).

The French expeditionary corps that captured Algiers in 1830 included a temporary regiment of mounted chasseurs (light cavalry), consisting of three squadrons, two of which were taken from the 17th Regiment of Mounted Chasseurs (one of which was equipped with lances) and from the 13th Regiment of Mounted Chasseurs. After the defeat of the Ottomans, the single squadron of the 13th Regiment was soon sent back to France, whereas the other two squadrons only returned to Europe in late 1831. In order to patrol Algiers effectively and to have a sufficient number of horsemen at their disposal, the French planned to raise local cavalry units made up of Algerian natives. On 9 October 1830, the French authorities decided to organize three squadrons of mounted Zouaves recruited from the Zwawa communities living

French Zouaves, with the typical green turban.

around Algiers. The Kabyle Zwawa tribes had provided excellent cavalry contingents to the Ottomans for many years, and the French were interested in employing them as mounted auxiliaries. The three new squadrons (later reduced to two) soon became known as the Chasseurs Algériens and adopted an early version of the future Spahis' uniform. Their members had a distinctive irregular nature and were armed with infantry muskets, since they were to operate more as mounted gendarmerie than true cavalry. Following the success of the Chasseurs Algériens, the French recruited another two units of native cavalry: one squadron of Chasseurs Numides and one squadron of guides. When the two remaining squadrons of metropolitan mounted chasseurs were sent back to France, however, it became clear that a new regular cavalry corps would have to be formed in Algeria. As a result, on 17 November 1831, the Chasseurs Algériens were disbanded and their members were united with those troopers of the 17th Mounted Chasseurs Regiment who volunteered to remain in Africa in order to create a new corps, the Chasseurs d'Afrique (African Chasseurs). Like the early Zouaves, they were a *corps mixte* comprising local recruits and French volunteers. The new corps was made up of two cavalry regiments, one stationed in Algiers and another in Oran. Like the early Zouaves, the African Chasseurs suffered from ill-discipline, and mutinied on two occasions during their early years. The 1st Regiment of African Chasseurs was quite easy to form, since it absorbed the two squadrons of Algerian Chasseurs. Originally it was to have just four squadrons, but these were augmented to eight by the end of 1832. The 2nd Regiment of African Chasseurs was organized more slowly, but it finally came to have six squadrons instead of the four originally planned. In December 1832, the French decided to raise a 3rd Regiment of African Chasseurs by merging the last two squadrons of the 1st Regiment with two squadrons of irregular cavalry which had recently been recruited.

On 27 July 1834, the French organized the first regular corps of native cavalrymen, known as the Spahis Réguliers d'Algiers, with the Algerian elements of the 1st Regiment of African Chasseurs (the former Chasseurs Algériens) detached from their parent unit in order to form the new corps. Following this organizational change, the 1st Regiment of African Chasseurs had five squadrons instead of the previous six. Over time, the number of Algerians within the Chasseurs d'Afrique increasingly dwindled; the native soldiers of the 1st Regiment became the Spahis Réguliers d'Algiers, the 2nd Regiment had just one squadron made up of Algerian elements and the 3rd Regiment consisted almost entirely of French volunteers. On 23 December 1839, the 6th Squadron of the 2nd Regiment and the 6th Squadron of the 3rd Regiment were joined together to form the new 4th Regiment of African Chasseurs. In consequence, by the beginning of 1840, each of the four units of Chasseurs d'Afrique had five squadrons; the native soldiers now made up two

French trooper of the Chasseurs d'Afrique, with the light blue tunic typical of this corps.

The French Army 101

French trooper of the Chasseurs d'Afrique, wearing campaign dress with short jacket.

squadrons in the 1st Regiment, two in the 2nd Regiment, one in the 3rd Regiment and one in the 4th Regiment. On 7 December 1841, with the creation of the Spahis and the complete reorganization of the native cavalry corps, the Chasseurs d'Afrique ceased to be a *corps mixte* and started to comprise only French volunteers. The four regiments of African Chasseurs replaced their native elements – who became part of the Spahis – with new French recruits, retaining their previous structure with six squadrons. With the reorganization of 1841–42, the Chasseurs d'Afrique lost their original mounted infantry character and became proper light cavalry. Each of the four regiments was stationed in a major Algerian city: the 1st at Algiers, the 2nd at Oran, the 3rd at Constantine and the 4th at Bône.

When the Crimean War broke out, the African Chasseurs had already earned a solid reputation as harsh fighters, between 1842 and 1845 having taken part in all the major engagements fought by the French against the insurgents of Abd al-Qādir. With the beginning of the new conflict, the four regiments of Chasseurs d'Afrique were each asked to provide four squadrons for the operations against the Russians. Each of them also formed a 7th and 8th Squadron, which remained in North Africa for the duration of hostilities and acted as depot units. The sixteen squadrons sent to the Crimean War were assembled into two temporary brigades: the 1st Brigade, consisting of the squadrons provided by the 1st and 4th Regiments, was commanded by General d'Allonville, while the 2nd Brigade, with the squadrons from the 2nd and 3rd Regiments, was led by General de Cassaignoles. Like the Zouaves, the African Chasseurs fought with great determination in Crimea. During the Battle of Balaclava, the 1st Brigade covered the retreat of what remained of the British Light Brigade.

Soon after their occupation of Algiers, the French, in addition to the regular Zouaves, started to recruit some local units of native auxiliaries from the former soldiers of Algeria's Ottoman garrison. These continued to be commanded by their own officers and did not wear uniforms, and as such were irregular corps. In February 1831, a first infantry company of Turks was organized in Oran from a few Janissaries who had decided to remain in Algeria, then a Turkish infantry battalion was formed in Bône in March 1832. During 1833, a second company was raised in Oran, which was followed by an entire battalion in early 1834. This new Turkish unit initially had three companies, which were later increased to five with the addition of the two independent companies that already existed in Oran. In 1837, however, the Turkish Battalion of Oran was disbanded due to its indiscipline, being replaced by a single infantry company that was made up of its most reliable elements. The Turkish Battalion of Bône performed quite well on several occasions and thus was retained in service by the French. On 17 November 1837, the unit recruited from the former Ottoman garrison of Bône was transformed into a half-battalion, but a new Turkish

Battalion of Constantine was created with some of its best elements. The latter unit had French officers and NCOs, differently from the others that had no French members. Initially no native units were raised from the province of Algiers, since it already provided native soldiers for the Zouaves, but four companies of Tirailleurs were raised in 1839 from the area around the Algerian capital. In January 1840, the French decided to raise a full battalion, known as the Bataillon de Tirailleurs indigènes d'Algiers et du Titteri, from Turks and Algerians who wished to serve under their flag. This new corps consisted of six companies, while the Turkish Battalion of Constantine had nine companies.

On 5 July 1840, another two light infantry companies were raised from the Algiers district and were united with the four units established in 1839 to form the new Native Half-Battalion of Titteri (a mountainous region near Algiers). This new formation of native infantry performed well on several occasions, showing the French their military potential, so in the autumn of 1841 it was decided that each of the three Algerian provinces (Algiers, Oran and Constantine) should have two battalions of native infantry. The Native Half-Battalion of Titteri was transformed into a battalion for the province of Algiers, and two new units (the Turkish Battalion of Mostaganem and Turkish Battalion of Oran) were raised in the province of Oran. All the new battalions had French superior officers and native junior officers. On 7 December 1841, General Bugeaud, appreciating the combat abilities of the Algerians, decided to transform the six existing battalions of irregular infantry into three battalions of regular infantry. These were known as Tirailleurs and were dressed similarly to the Zouaves, who sent their remaining native elements to the new Tirailleur battalions. The Bataillon de Tirailleurs indigènes d'Algiers et du Titteri was joined with the Native Battalion of Titteri to form the new 1st Tirailleur Battalion of Algiers (with six companies), the Turkish Battalion of Mostaganem and Turkish Battalion of Oran became the 2nd Tirailleur Battalion of Oran (with four companies), and the Turkish Battalion of Bône and Turkish Battalion of Constantine formed the 3rd Tirailleur Battalion of Constantine (with eight companies).

With the outbreak of the Crimean War, the Tirailleurs were called to serve overseas for the first time. In the spring of 1854, each of the three battalions – which were now all structured on eight companies – was asked to provide six companies to form the Régiment de Marche de Tirailleurs Algériens. This unit, consisting of two battalions with nine companies each, fought with distinction in several engagements: the Alma (20 September 1854), Inkerman (5 November 1854) and Malakoff (7 September 1855). While in Crimea they earned the nickname of *Turcos* (Turks), since the Russians judged from their oriental-style uniforms that they were part of the Ottoman Army. Meanwhile, on 9 January 1855, one new battalion of Tirailleurs

Soldiers of the Tirailleurs Algériens, whose uniform was very similar to that worn by the Zouaves but was light blue.

was raised from each Algerian province in order to replace the native soldiers who were fighting in Crimea. Before the conflict with Russia came to an end, on 18 October 1855, it was decided to unite the two battalions of each province to form three regiments of Tirailleurs, each consisting of three battalions with six companies.

Before the arrival of the French, the Ottoman garrison of Algeria comprised a number of professional cavalry who were known as *Sipahi*, a term transformed into 'Spahis' by the French, which continued to be used after the French conquest of Algiers to indicate locally recruited native horsemen. Before leaving North Africa after the July Revolution of 1830, General Bourmont, who commanded the French invasion of Algiers, decided to include two squadrons of native *Sipahi* in the French forces garrisoning Algiers. His successor, General Clauzel, confirmed this decision, leading to the creation of three squadrons of Chasseurs Algériens (later reduced to two). As we have already seen, these were soon absorbed into the newly formed Chasseurs d'Afrique, which was initially a *corps mixte*. The former *Sipahi*, however, were not particularly enthusiastic about serving in the African Chasseurs since they were not used to strict military discipline and wanted to be commanded by their own officers. As a result, on 10 September 1834, the French raised a new native cavalry corps known as the Spahis réguliers d'Algiers. This consisted of four squadrons with 200 men each, and absorbed the former members of the Chasseurs Algériens who had been included in the 1st Regiment of African Chasseurs. On 12 August 1836, the Spahis réguliers d'Algiers were expanded from four to six squadrons. Meanwhile, similar corps of regular native cavalry were also formed in Bône (on 10 June 1835) and Oran (on 12 August 1836). These had four squadrons each and soon proved they were reliable soldiers like the unit organized in Algiers. During this early period, the French also recruited some irregular contingents of native horsemen: a single cavalry squadron made up of Turkish soldiers in Bône and a mixed unit (800 infantry and 200 cavalry) in Constantine. In September 1840, several new irregular corps of native cavalry were formed, with one at Algiers, one at Sétif and three in the province of Constantine. Meanwhile, the French had also organized a native gendarmerie, made up of horsemen and tasked with patrolling the countryside of Algiers. Created in 1836, they received the denomination of Gendarmes Maures (Moorish Gendarmes). Originally structured on independent platoons attached to the French units of gendarmerie, the unit was reorganized as follows on 5 July 1840: two squadrons in the province of Algiers (one patrolling the city and one the countryside), one platoon in Constantine, one platoon in Bône and one platoon in Philippeville. The officers of the Gendarmes Maures were all French and the unit performed well as an auxiliary police force.

On 7 December 1841, recognizing that the Spahis had a great military potential, the French decided to improve the organization of their locally recruited native cavalry. The Moorish Gendarmes and units of irregular Spahis were all disbanded in order to form a single and unified corps of regular Spahis. The new formation consisted of twenty independent squadrons, each of which had four French superior

Trooper of the Spahis Algériens, wearing the traditional red uniform of his corps.

officers, three Algerian junior officers, twenty French NCOs and 173 Algerian junior NCOs or troopers. Overall command of the Spahis was given to the famous General Yusuf, a Corsican – originally named Joseph Vantini – who had spent most of his

The French Army 107

Trooper of the Spahis Algériens in the Crimean winter, wearing his long red 'burnous' cloak.

life in Tunisia and who had joined the French military during their early conquest of Algeria. Yusuf was a Muslim, had an extensive knowledge of native traditions and spoke several local languages, and consequently was particularly loved by his men, proving extremely valuable for the French. The twenty squadrons of Spahis were distributed as follows: five in the province of Algiers, nine in the province of

Constantine and ten in the province of Oran. On 21 July 1845, the organization based on independent squadrons was abandoned and the various units were assembled together to form three regiments: the 1st Spahis Regiment of Algiers, 2nd Spahis Regiment of Oran and 3rd Spahis Regiment of Constantine. Each of these consisted of six squadrons. One platoon of the 1st Regiment was detached from its parent unit and sent to Senegal, where it provided cadres for the formation of the new Squadron of Senegalese Spahis.

At the outbreak of the Crimean War, the Spahis were asked to form a single Escadron de Marche or temporary squadron, which was made up of volunteers from the three existing regiments. This unit did not see much combat against the Russians, actin instead as the mounted escort of the French expeditionary force's commander-in-chief. On 24 June 1854, the French decided to raise a new unit of native cavalry, known as the Spahis d'Orient, from the many *bashi-bazouks* (irregular fighters) who were available in the Ottoman Empire. General Yusuf was ordered to form a semi-regular military corps from these undisciplined soldiers of fortune; the original plan was to form eight regiments of Spahis d'Orient with four squadrons each, but in the end not a single squadron became operative and the whole project was cancelled in August 1854 (after most of the *bashi-bazouks* deserted with the modern weapons that they had just received from the French).

In addition to the above, the Army of Africa also comprised the famous Foreign Legion. During the Napoleonic Wars, the French Army had included a large number of foreign units, deploying four infantry regiments entirely made up of foreigners. With the restoration of the Bourbons, all foreign units of the French Army were immediately disbanded, but a large number of soldiers of fortune (mostly from Switzerland and Germany) decided to remain in France and swore loyalty to the new political regime. As a result, on 6 September 1815, a Loyal Foreign Legion was formed within the royal army to unite in a single unit all the foreigners in the French infantry. This corps comprised soldiers of many nationalities and became known as the Hohenlohe Regiment in 1821 after the name of its commander (the German Prince of Hohenlohe). After 1815, the French Royal Guard also included some foreign soldiers assembled into two elite regiments of infantry. In 1831, following the revolution of the previous year, the Hohenlohe Regiment and the Swiss regiments of the Royal Guard were all disbanded, the French populace considering them a threat to their freedom as a weapon in the hands of the monarchy. In 1830, however, France had launched its new colonial adventure in Algeria and thus was in search of veteran soldiers who would be available for service overseas. Most of the French conscripts disliked service in North Africa due to the harsh local climate and the presence of many deadly diseases; as a result, rates of desertion were particularly high in Algeria. To solve this problem and to provide new employment to the soldiers of the disbanded foreign units, on 10 May 1831 the French government decided to create the Foreign Legion. The new unit comprised professional soldiers who would serve only outside the metropolitan territories of France. It consisted of seven battalions (later reduced to six) of infantry, each of which was made up of soldiers from the same nation: the first three battalions consisted of Swiss and Germans, the 4th Battalion of Spaniards, the 5th of Italians, the 6th of Dutch and Belgians and the 7th of Poles. During 1835 and 1836, the Foreign Legion was sent to Spain to support the local government (which was allied with France) in its struggle with the Carlist rebels. These operations in Spain were incredibly bloody for the corps, which was completely annihilated. Consequently, in 1836, a new Foreign Legion with five battalions was gradually formed in Algeria. In early 1841, the corps was greatly enlarged and was reorganized on two infantry regiments with three battalions each. The 1st Regiment consisted of volunteers from northern Europe, and the 2nd Regiment of volunteers from southern Europe. At the start of the Crimean War, the two regiments of the Foreign Legion were ordered to form four temporary marching battalions made up of volunteers, which were sent to fight against the Russians. The four units of legionaries were involved in all the major battles in which the French Army fought and were considered – by several contemporary observers – as its best units. In March 1855, due to the war effort, it was decided to expand the two infantry regiments of the Foreign Legion to four battalions each, although the number of companies in each battalion was simultaneously reduced to six.

When France entered the Crimean War, Napoleon III experienced more or less the same problems as the British since despite having a larger army than the British he needed more professional soldiers willing to serve in a far-flung and inhospitable region of Europe. Seeing the success of the Foreign Legion, Napoleon III decided in January 1855 to raise a second Foreign Legion made up entirely of Swiss volunteers. As we have already seen, Switzerland had always produced many mercenaries willing to serve around Europe, with the British also deciding to raise their own Swiss Legion during the Crimean War. Swiss professional soldiers had served in the ranks of the French Army for centuries, since the early days of the Renaissance, and until the revolution of 1830 the French Royal Guard had included two regiments of Swiss infantry. Before becoming emperor, Napoleon III had spent some time living in Switzerland and had served in the military of one of the local cantons, and he thus understood that Swiss soldiers had a great military potential due to their discipline and determination. He decided to form an entire Swiss Brigade, which was officially constituted on 17 January 1855. The new corps was known as the II Foreign Legion, the existing multinational Foreign Legion receiving the official denomination of the

I Foreign Legion. The Swiss Legion consisted of two line infantry regiments, each with two battalions of six companies, plus an independent battalion of Tirailleurs (riflemen) with ten companies. The professional Swiss soldiers were renowned as light infantrymen, armed with rifled carbines and capable of employing effective skirmishing tactics, so Napoleon III wanted to include a battalion of these light troops in his infantry. Overall command of the new Swiss Legion was given to Ulrich Ochsenbein, a close friend of the emperor, who was a skilled military commander as well as a politician. The depot of the new corps was located in Besançon, 40 miles from the Swiss border; most of the recruits for the Swiss Legion came from the French-speaking cantons of Switzerland. The soldiers of the new II Legion were dressed exactly like those of the veteran I Legion, but their uniforms were of a distinctive dark green colour instead of the usual dark blue. Against Napoleon III's expectations, recruiting operations for the Swiss Legion were difficult from the outset, largely due to the fact that the new authorities of the centralized Switzerland created in 1852 wished to prevent foreign powers from recruiting large mercenary contingents in the cantons. By the end of the Crimean War, the 1st Line Regiment had organized just seven companies, the 2nd Line Regiment four companies and the Tirailleur Battalion only three companies. These never saw action, the Swiss Legion being officially disbanded on 25 June 1856. A few months later, in order to replenish the heavy losses suffered by the I Foreign Legion in Crimea, Napoleon decided to completely reorganize his foreign troops on two regiments: the 1st Foreign Regiment (made up of former members of the disbanded Swiss Legion) and the 2nd Foreign Regiment (comprising soldiers from the former I Foreign Legion who had remained in Algeria during the Crimean War). The 1st Foreign Regiment retained a distinct Swiss nature (and distinctive green uniforms) until 1859.

The Foreign Legion and Zouaves were not the only corps of the Army of Africa entirely made up of white soldiers – there were also the Battalions of African Light Infantry. These were created on 13 June 1832 as a semi-penal military corps, their rankers chosen from soldiers of the metropolitan army who had been condemned to correctional penalties or from civilian convicts who upon completing their term of imprisonment still had obligations for compulsory military service. Since 1818, the French Army had included some disciplinary companies of fusiliers or sappers, but these had been mostly employed as auxiliary corps rather than combat units; the French authorities were worried about the idea of arming *rabistes* (hungry men) who had been punished by military justice. With the conquest of Algiers, these ex-deserters or undisciplined soldiers had an opportunity to fight again for their country but away from their homeland. The African Light Infantry initially consisted of two battalions with eight companies each (increased to ten in 1834), which were sent to

The French Army 111

NCO of the Tirailleur Battalion of the Swiss Legion in French service, with the dark green campaign dress of his corps.

Tataouine on the border between Algeria and Tunisia. This was one of the most arid and hostile places in North Africa, where no regular soldier wanted to serve. Once in Algeria, the members of the African Light Infantry earned the nickname of *Les Joyeux* (The Happy Ones); they were, in fact, not particularly enthusiast about their new life in North Africa. In September 1833, a 3rd Bataillon d'infanterie légère d'Afrique was formed, and from 1836 civilian convicts who had completed their period of compulsory military service also started to be admitted into the ranks of the African Light Infantry. Initially, the three battalions were mostly employed as auxiliary units of sappers, but several of their companies later participated in combat operations. The 10th Company of the 1st Battalion, in particular, distinguished itself in 1840 during the Battle of Mazagran, when *Les Joyeux* defended their positions with great courage from assaults by 1,200 Algerian fighters loyal to Abd al-Qādir. During the Crimean War, two temporary companies of African Light Infantry, made up of volunteers from the three existing battalions, fought against the Russians.

Chapter 3

The Russian Army

The Russian Army of 1853 was the largest military force in the world, potentially able to mobilize 1,365,786 men in case of war. These were structured on four different organizations that would perform distinctive tasks: 678,201 soldiers of the regular Russian Army, 212,433 soldiers of the reserve army, 144,937 soldiers of the interior forces and 242,203 soldiers of the irregular forces. This impressive manpower was the result of Russia's enormous territorial extent and vast population. However, it should be noted that mobilizing these forces and concentrating them in a single point of the Russian Empire was practically impossible because they were scattered around a huge area that extended from Poland to Alaska. The Russians had created a western-style army only during the early decades of the eighteenth century, when Peter the Great menaced Swedish expansionism in the Baltic. As a result, the Russian Army was quite 'young' compared to those of the other major powers. Nevertheless, the quality of the regular Russian military increased dramatically during the eighteenth century, with the Russian Army largely responsible for Napoleon's decisive defeats between 1812 and 1814. After having suffered many reversals against the French from 1805–07, the Russians expanded their armed forces in an incredible way by forming dozens of new units and mobilizing a major part of their military potential. At the Battle of Borodino in 1812, they proved to Napoleon that they were able to face his multinational army of 600,000 troops on almost equal terms. After abandoning Moscow, the French were harassed by Cossacks and other mounted soldiers of Russia's enormous irregular forces, which were still equipped with medieval weapons yet were considered – by many contemporary observers – to be the best cavalry of the world. The Russians played a prominent role during the German Campaign of 1813 and the French Campaign of 1814, which broke the power of Napoleon. Consequently, Russia emerged from the Congress of Vienna as one of Europe's major powers.

The Russians were governed by an absolute monarchy and lived in a state that had no industry to speak of. Their country still had laws based on feudal principles and most of them (many millions) were poor peasants who played no active role in the political life of their nation. Despite this, the Russian monarchs feared no enemy thanks to the huge size of their armed forces. Their regular and reserve armies were well trained and well equipped, while their interior forces were capable of suppressing any potential peasant revolt and their irregular forces had already terrorized much of Europe during the Napoleonic Wars. The Cossacks and the many other auxiliaries from the heartland of Asia were a peculiarity of the Russian Army, since no other European power could count on such a large native cavalry. The Cossacks and the other auxiliaries were the last remnants of the pre-1700 Russian Army, but while they could not conduct a campaign against a westernized army on their own, they could perform various kinds of operations – such as scouting and skirmishing – better than any other horsemen. After victory in the Napoleonic Wars, Russia became an ever-expanding empire. In Europe, it was given Poland and Finland by the Congress of Vienna and thus started to play a prominent political role also in the central part of the continent. In the Balkans and the Caucasus, Russian lands bordered those of the Ottomans. The Russians, well aware of the Turks' severe internal difficulties, had as their main political objective that of causing the collapse of the Ottoman Empire in order to annex more Balkan and Caucasian lands. Russia was also interested in expanding towards India from its vast possessions in Central Asia (which reached the borders of Afghanistan) and towards the northern regions of China (Mongolia and Manchuria). The Russians had more than a foothold in North America, where they had colonized Alaska and had plans to move southwards along the coastline of California.

After 1815, to pursue their expansionist ambitions, the Russians fought several minor wars and achieved great success. They launched an invasion of the Caucasus in 1817, with the objective of submitting forever the native communities that had never accepted Russia's predominance over their lands. This conflict, known as the Caucasian War, lasted until 1864 and was extremely costly for the Russians, who lost thousands of men before overcoming the Muslims of the mountainous region. The local communities employed effective guerrilla tactics and had an extensive knowledge of their homelands, but the numerical superiority of the Russians was eventually decisive in determining the outcome of the conflict. This was a real test for the Russian Army, which experienced serious difficulties in the Caucasus. Between 1826 and 1828, Russia was at war with Persia over possession of the eastern portion of the southern Caucasus; while in 1828 and 1829 the Russians fought the Ottomans for dominance over the Balkan principalities of Moldavia and Wallachia. Both conflicts ended in victory for Russia, neither the Persians nor the Turks having regular forces that could face the Russians on equal terms. Meanwhile, with the objective of weakening the Ottomans and expanding towards the southern Balkans to reach the Mediterranean, Russia had strongly supported the Greeks in their war of independence and had destroyed – together with the naval forces of Britain and France – the Ottoman fleet at the Battle of Navarino (1827). Poland revolted against the Russians from 1830–31, in the hope of regaining its former independence, but the Polish patriots were eventually crushed by superior Russian troops and the previous limited autonomy of their country was extinguished. From 1839–41, the Russians intervened inside the borders of the Ottoman Empire to repulse an Egyptian invasion that was threatening to sieze Constantinople. Finally, in 1849, Russia played a decisive role in defeating the Hungarian uprising that had almost annihilated the Austrian Empire. Hungary had revolted against Austria and claimed independence, defeating the Austrians on several occasions, and it was only thanks to Russia's intervention that the patriots were defeated. Russia's participation in the conflict had been inspired by its desire to prevent the outbreak of major uprisings among the populations of Eastern Europe that had been placed under foreign rule by the Congress of Vienna (notably the Poles and Hungarians). In consequence of its recent activities, the Russian Army of 1853 was a very experienced military force that had fought against many different enemies on various kinds of terrain. Compared with the British Army, for example, it had much more recent large-scale combat experience. However, the expansionism of Russia had made the country quite isolated diplomatically, since its traditional allies – Austria and Prussia – had started to fear that the empire governed from Moscow could become too powerful.

Imperial Guard

The Russian Regular Army included a very large Imperial Guard, which had been created by Peter the Great during the early eighteenth century. Peter the Great initiated the westernization of the Russian military by forming a miniature army with western-style training and uniforms. This experimental force was soon transformed into two regiments of elite infantry, which acted as a model for the modernization of the whole Russian line infantry: the Preobrazhenskii Regiment and Semenovskii Regiment. Over several decades the Russian Imperial Guard was greatly enlarged with the addition of new units and started to comprise corps of every branch of service. It became an elite 'army within an army', tasked with defending the Romanov dynasty. New units of the Imperial Guard tended not to be raised from scratch, but consisted of line regiments that – due to their valour in battle or high degree of loyalty – were given the privilege of being transformed into guard corps, a situation which happened quite often during the Napoleonic Wars. The guard regiments enjoyed a series of privileges, such as receiving higher pay and having better living conditions than the line units.

In 1853, the infantry of the Russian Imperial Guard consisted of the following twelve regiments (ordered according to their seniority): the Preobrazhenskii, Semenovskii, Izmailovskii, Grenaderskii, Pavlovskii, Yegerskii, Finlyandskii, Litovskii, Volynskii, Moskovskii, His Majesty the Emperor of Austria's Regiment and His Majesty the King of Prussia's Regiment. The Preobrazhenskii and Semenovskii regiments were the oldest units, having been formed in 1683, and had already been westernized by the beginning of the eighteenth century. The Izmailovskii Regiment was raised in 1730 as the personal foot guard of Empress Anne. The Grenaderskii Regiment was a heavy infantry regiment of grenadiers that was formed in 1756 as the 1st Grenadier Regiment of the Russian infantry. Having fought with distinction on several occasions, in 1775 the unit was admitted into the ranks of the Imperial Guard. The Pavlovskii Regiment was also a grenadier unit, having been created in 1790 by assembling together several companies of grenadiers from line foot regiments. The Yegerskii Regiment had a peculiar history, since it was a unit of riflemen. The Russian Army did not comprise any independent corps of light infantry until 1792, and none of its regular units were equipped with rifles. In that year, however, following the example of other European armies, the Russians raised two experimental companies of riflemen. These, after undergoing intensive training,

Russian private of the Preobrazhenskii Regiment of the Imperial Guard. The mitre grenadier cap was typical of this unit, which had adopted it since its creation by Peter the Great.

performed very well during exercises and were soon consolidated into a battalion of riflemen that became part of the Imperial Guard in 1796. In 1806, the battalion was expanded to become a regiment. The name of the unit derived from the German word *Jäger* (Hunter), which was used during the eighteenth century to identify light infantry formations equipped with rifled carbines. Prussian military influence over the Russian Army was particularly strong during the eighteenth century, especially after the ascendancy of Frederick the Great. Tsar Peter III, who ruled for just a few months during 1762, was a German prince and a personal admirer of the Prussian militarism. He introduced several typically German elements to the Russian military and temporarily attached some corps from his own army of the Duchy of Holstein-Gottorp to the Russian Army. The Prussian influence over Russian forces persisted during and after the Napoleonic Wars, being still clearly visible in 1853. The Finlyandskii Regiment, known as the Finlandian Regiment, was formed in 1806 by converting a battalion of the militia and was transformed into a guard regiment in 1811. The Litowski Regiment was also called the Lithuanian Regiment and was formed in 1811 from one of the battalions of the Preobrazhenskii Regiment, while the Volynskii Regiment, known as the Volhynian Regiment (Volhynia being a region between Poland and Ukraine), was formed in 1806 by converting a battalion of the militia, being made into a guard regiment in 1817. The Moskovskii Regiment was created in 1817 by detaching two battalions from the Litowski Regiment. The two regiments titled after the monarchs of Austria and Prussia, who were their honorary commanders and close allies of the Russian Tsar, were given their peculiar denominations in 1814 to celebrate the victories of the Allies over Napoleon; they were admitted into the ranks of the Imperial Guard only in 1831.

Of the twelve foot regiments of the Imperial Guard, only two could be defined as proper grenadier units (the Grenaderskii and Pavlovskii), and only one was of light infantry (the Yegerskii). The foot units of the Imperial Guard were assembled into three divisions, each of which consisted of four regiments. Individual regiments had three battalions, with each battalion having four companies: one of grenadiers and three of musketeers in the line regiments, one of grenadiers and three of fusiliers in the grenadier regiments, and one of carabiniers and three of jägers in the light regiments. Since musketeers and fusiliers were two names meaning the same thing, in practice there was no difference between the grenadier regiments and the standard line regiments except for some elements of the uniform. The companies of grenadiers, musketeers and fusiliers had 250 men each, while those of carabiniers and jägers had 180 men each. Attached to the three divisions of guard infantry were two independent battalions: one of riflemen and another of naval infantry. The rifle battalion had a unique history, being the only 'national' unit of the Russian Imperial Guard and consisting entirely of Finnish soldiers. Finland was annexed to the Russian Empire, after centuries of Swedish domination, after the Congress of Vienna. The country was administered as a semi-autonomous Grand Duchy and had to raise six battalions of riflemen for its defence. The inhabitants of Finland were used to very harsh living conditions and most of the Finnish farmers were also excellent hunters, meaning that Finland could potentially provide some excellent light infantry to Russia. In 1817, a new Finnish infantry unit – known as the Training Battalion or Helsinki Battalion – was raised, which differently from the existing ones, could be required to serve outside the borders of Finland. In 1829, the Helsinki Battalion was ordered to train with and became part of the foot regiments of the Russian Imperial Guard. The six battalions of Finnish riflemen were disbanded in 1830, so the Finnish Guards' Rifle Battalion (the former Helsinki Battalion) remained as the only Finnish unit of the Russian Army. It consisted entirely of volunteers and was attached to the 2nd Division of the Imperial Guard's infantry. During 1854 and 1855, with Finland's Baltic coast being menaced by British and French forces, the Russians raised nine rifle battalions from the Grand Duchy, but these were soon demobilized at the end of the Crimean War.

The Imperial Guard's battalion of naval infantry, officially known as the Guard Crew, was formed in 1810 and consisted of eight active companies plus one company of rowers and one squad of gunners. It was tasked with acting as the crew for the ships of the Romanov Imperial family, but its members could also perform as normal infantry. The corps was clearly inspired

Russian NCO of the Litowski Regiment, Imperial Guard. The red plastron on the front of the tunic was worn by several foot units of the Imperial Guard.

Russian privates of the Yegerski Regiment (left) and Finlyandskii Regiment (right) of the Imperial Guard. The additional lace on collar and cuffs was a distinctive element of the guard units' dress.

Russian officer of the Company of Palace Grenadiers, Imperial Guard. This small elite unit was the only one in the Russian Army to wear a bearskin in French style.

Jäger of the Finnish Rifle Battalion (left) and marine of the Guard Crew (right), Imperial Guard. White trousers were worn by all foot units during summer.

by Napoleon's Marines of the Imperial Guard and wore a distinctive uniform. For protection of the Tsar's person there also was a small independent unit of foot lifeguards, the Company of Palace Grenadiers. This was created in 1827 and consisted of veteran soldiers selected from the foot regiments of the Imperial Guard. It was tasked with guarding the Imperial Palace and the people who lived in it, hence its denomination.

On paper, the foot units of the Russian Imperial Guard formed an impressive combat force, but they did not play a significant role in the Crimean War since the Russians always preferred to preserve them in order to have a large and loyal contingent to rely on in case of internal revolts.

The cavalry of the Russian Imperial Guard was extremely numerous, consisting of several units with different specializations. Differently from the infantry, it comprised various national corps recruited from the ethnic minorities of the Russian state. The Russian Imperial Guard comprised the following sixteen formations: the Konnyi, Kavalergardskii, Kirasirskii, Kirasirskii Eya Velichestva Imperatritsa, Dragunskii, Konno-Grenaderskii, Ulanskii, Ulanskii Ego Imperatorskago Vysochestva Tsesarevicha, Gusarskii, Grodnenskii Gusarskii, Kazachii, Kazachii Ego Imperatorskago Vysochestva Tsesarevicha, Chernomorskii Eskadron, Uralskaya Sotnya, His Majesty's Own Cossack Escort and Zhandarmskii Polueskadron. The Konnyi Regiment, or Life Guard Regiment, was the most ancient mounted unit of the Russian Imperial Guard, being raised as early as 1721 by Peter the Great, who wanted a heavy cavalry unit to act as his mounted bodyguard, following the example of his sworn enemy the Swedish king. The new unit was formed by merging two squadrons that had already been formed by Russian commanders to act as their escorts and one squadron of mounted gendarmes that garrisoned the newly built Imperial capital of St Petersburg. From its foundation, the Konnyi Regiment was given a distinctive and elegant uniform that was similar to that worn by the contemporary French musketeers. The Kavalergardskii Regiment, or Chevalier Guard Regiment, was another heavy cavalry unit tasked with acting as the mounted bodyguard of the Romanovs, but differently from the Konnyi Regiment it consisted from its foundation of noblemen from Russia's leading aristocratic families. Raised in 1724, the corps was temporarily disbanded several times during the eighteenth century for economic reasons and consisted of a single squadron until 1800. In that year it was transformed into a regiment of three squadrons and became officially part of the Imperial Guard. Both the Konnyi Regiment and the Kavalergardskii Regiment were akin to cuirassiers, but their members did not wear metal cuirasses. The Kirasirskii Regiment, or Cuirassier Regiment, was raised as a dragoon unit in 1706 and was given cuirasses only in 1732. It became part of the Imperial Guard in 1762 due to its loyalty towards the dynasty. The Kirasirskii Eya Velichestya Imperatritsa Regiment, or Her Majesty the Empress' Own Cuirassier Regiment, was raised as a dragoon unit in 1704 and given cuirasses in 1733, then in 1764 it became part of the Imperial Guard. The Dragunskii Regiment, or Dragoon Regiment, had a peculiar history, being raised in 1814 from the best soldiers of the Russian line cavalry who had distinguished themselves during the campaigns fought against Napoleon. Initially it was a corps of mounted chasseurs, but it was always part of the Imperial Guard. After performing well during the Polish uprising of 1830–31, the regiment was transformed into a dragoon unit in 1833.

Russian NCO of the Kavalergardskii Regiment of the Imperial Guard. Note the double-headed eagle on top of the helmet (a symbol of Russia) and the Star of St Andrew embroidered on the chest (the symbol of Russia's patron saint).

Russian trooper of the Dragunskii Regiment, Imperial Guard. He is wearing the new double-breasted tunic introduced by the dress regulations of 1855; this is in the black colour that was distinctive of the regiment.

Russian trooper of the Konno-Grenaderskii Regiment, Imperial Guard. Note the strange headgear: a metal helmet surmounted by a massive bearskin.

The Konno-Grenaderskii Regiment, or Mounted Grenadiers Regiment, was created in 1809, already as part of the Imperial Guard. Until 1831 it was a regiment of dragoons; in that year it received the new denomination of Mounted Grenadiers but in practice it retained its dragoon features. The Ulanskii Regiment, or Uhlan Regiment, was formed in 1803 and became part of the Imperial Guard in 1812. In Russia, the term 'uhlan' was used to indicate lancers, exactly as in the Austrian Empire and the Kingdom of Prussia. During 1817, from some squadrons of the unit that were garrisoned in Poland, the new Ulanskii Ego Imperatorskago Vysochestva Tsesarevicha Regiment, or His Majesty the Tsarevich's Own Uhlan Regiment, was created. This new corps was the personal cavalry unit of the heir to the Russian throne (the Tsarevich). The Gusarskii Regiment, or Hussar Regiment, was created in 1775 and initially consisted of just a single squadron, mostly recruited from Balkan soldiers who had already served as light cavalry in other armies. Between 1796 and 1798 the Hussars of the Imperial Guard (now consisting of two squadrons) were temporarily merged with two squadrons of Cossacks. In 1798, this unit was split in two and the Gusarskii Regiment was officially created. The Grodnenskii Gusarskii Regiment, or Grodno's Hussar Regiment, was raised in 1824, mostly from Poles who were loyal to the Russians. It always had guard status. The Kazachii Regiment, or Cossack Regiment, became an autonomous unit in 1798, after having consisted of just two squadrons – that were attached to the Hussars of the Imperial Guard – from 1796–98. The corps was considered one of the best units of the Imperial Guard since its members were recruited from the Don Cossacks, who were the most powerful Cossack community of Russia and the most loyal to the Romanovs. From 1832, a squadron of Crimean Tatars (Muslim descendants of the Mongols who had settled in Ukraine) was attached to the regiment.

The Kazachii Ego Imperatorskago Vysochestva Tsesarevicha Regiment, or His Majesty the Tsarevich's Own Cossack Regiment, had a peculiar history. Around the middle of the seventeenth century, the powerful Zaporozhian Cossacks living in Ukraine established a centralized state over the vast plains that they controlled, but spent most of their time fighting against the strong enemies that surrounded them: the Poles in the west, the Ottomans to the south and the Russians in the east. Russian influence over the Zaporozhian Cossacks became increasingly significant, to the point that their partly modernized state was progressively transformed into a Russian protectorate. The Zaporozhian nation was known as the Cossack Hetmanate, since it was guided by a supreme leader known as Hetman. It was protected, by the mid-eighteenth century, by guard units that were trained and uniformed in western style; the rest of the Zaporozhian forces were organized in regiments but still fought in their traditional Cossack fashion. In 1775, the

Russian trooper of the Ulanskii Regiment, Imperial Guard. The uniform is of clear Polish cut, with czapska squared headgear and kurtka tunic.

Russian trooper of the Ulanskii Ego Imperatorskago Vysochestva Tsesarevicha Regiment, Imperial Guard. This unit had silver lace in order to be easily distinguishable from the other lancer corps of the Imperial Guard that had golden lace.

Russian trooper of the Gusarskii Regiment of the Imperial Guard. The colours of this unit's uniform had not changed since the days of the Napoleonic Wars.

Russian troopers of the Kazachii Ego Imperatorskago Vysochestva Tsesarevicha Regiment (left) and Kazachii Regiment (right), Imperial Guard. The first unit was dressed in medium blue, the second in red.

Officer of the Tatar Squadron attached to the Kazachii Regiment, Imperial Guard. Note the peculiar Tatar headgear.

Cossack Hetmanate was officially absorbed into the Russian Empire and ceased to be an independent political entity; most of its military, both regular and irregular, became part of the Russian Army. The political figure of the Hetman, however, continued to represent the unity and culture of the Zaporozhian Cossacks. In 1775, the Russians decided to assemble the best elements from the disbanded Zaporozhian military to form a new Cossack unit, which became known as the Hetman Regiment. This proved an excellent corps, which in 1829 was made part of the Imperial Guard. Two years later it received its definitive official denomination. The Chernomorskii Eskadron, or Black Sea Squadron, was recruited from the Cossack communities living on the western coastline of the Caucasus in 1828 and was attached to the Kazachii Regiment. The Uralskaya Sotnia, or Ural Cossack Company, was formed in 1798 and consisted of Ural Cossacks. It was attached to the Kazachii Ego Imperatorskago Vysochestva Tsesarevicha Regiment, but unlike its parent unit was tasked with performing guard duties at the Imperial Palace in St Petersburg. His Majesty's Own Cossack Escort was the most colourful unit of the Imperial Guard's cavalry, consisting of Circassians from the Caucasus who had a fanatical loyalty towards the Tsar. The Circassians were the fiercest enemies of the Russians in the Caucasus and were the last to surrender in 1864 when the region was conquered by Russia. From the early years of war in the Caucasus, the Russians therefore tried to

The Russian Army 131

Officer (left) and trooper (right) of the Chernomorskii Eskadron, Imperial Guard. The influence of the Caucasian national costume is clearly visible in this uniform, which includes the *papacha* headgear covered with fur and the *gazyrs* breast pockets.

obtain the loyalty of some Circassians in order to form a unit symbolizing the future submission of Circassia to the Tsar. In 1839, while combat operations in the Caucasus were at an early stage, a squadron of Circassians was finally raised. This was given the special task of escorting the personal convoy of the Tsar whenever it moved across Russia (something that happened quite frequently). The Circassians were audacious fighters and had a quite picturesque appearance, wearing full chainmail armour and being armed with composite bows. The Zhandarmskii

Circassian trooper of His Majesty Own's Cossack Escort of the Imperial Guard. This unit had one of the most picturesque uniforms of the whole Russian Army.

Circassian trooper of His Majesty's Own Cossack Escort, Imperial Guard. He is wearing the traditional military dress of his people that included helmet and chainmail.

Russian officer (centre) and troopers of the Zhandarmskii Polueskadron, Imperial Guard.

Polueskadron, or Gendarmerie Half-Squadron, was created in 1816 to act as the mounted military police of the Russian Imperial Guard. Its members were all experienced soldiers from the ranks of other Imperial Guard mounted formations. All the horse regiments of the Imperial Guard had six squadrons each, and each squadron consisted of 150 troopers.

The Russian Imperial Guard also included some artillery units and small technical formations which were attached to the infantry divisions. The guard artillery consisted of three foot brigades and one mounted corps. The 1st Foot Artillery Brigade, created in 1816, was attached to the 1st Infantry Division; the 2nd Foot Artillery Brigade, formed in 1816, was part of the 2nd Infantry Division; and the 3rd Foot Artillery Brigade, formed in 1831 by merging several existing batteries, was attached to the 3rd Infantry Division. Each brigade comprised two batteries of heavy artillery and one of light artillery. A second battery of light artillery was added to each of the four brigades in 1854. The Horse Artillery Corps was created in 1805 as a single battery, expanding to comprise two batteries in 1811. In 1814, the Horse Artillery Corps was restructured on one heavy battery and two light batteries; a third light battery was added in 1817. A fourth light battery was formed in 1830 from the best elements of the Don Cossacks' mounted artillery, who had fought with great distinction in 1828 and 1829 against the Ottomans. Consequently, by 1854, the Horse Artillery Corps consisted of one heavy battery and four light batteries. From 1812, the Russian Imperial Guard also had a Sapper Battalion, which was formed from the best elements of the newly created line sapper units. In 1854, this battalion consisted of two companies of sappers and two of miners. From 1819, the Imperial Guard also featured a curious unit known as the Squadron of Mounted Pioneers, made up of mounted pioneers who had a higher degree of mobility than their foot equivalents. The Sapper Battalion and Mounted Pioneer Squadron were coordinated by the Engineer Corps of the Imperial Guard, a staff consisting of officers with specific technical skills. The Imperial Guard also had four train battalions, which were tasked with transporting the materiel of the four main artillery units, along with several auxiliary units: one garrison battalion performing static defence duties and fifteen companies of invalids (members of the guard who were no longer fit for active military service).

Infantry

The Russian regular infantry consisted of three main components: the heavy infantry, line infantry and light infantry. The heavy infantry was organized as a separate Grenadier Corps, which had elite status and organizationally was placed halfway between the foot units of the Imperial Guard and those of the line infantry. Since the days of Peter the Great, the heavy infantry of the grenadiers had always been an autonomous component of the Russian Army, having its own independent regiments. After most other European armies ceased to have autonomous grenadier corps and started to include grenadier companies inside their standard line infantry regiments, the Russians retained their independent grenadier regiments. By 1854, there were twelve of these regiments, organized exactly like the foot regiments of the Imperial Guard in three divisions with two brigades each. A single brigade comprised two regiments and each regiment consisted of three battalions. A grenadier battalion

Uniforms of the Russian infantry (from left to right): line infantryman with summer dress, light infantryman with campaign dress and line infantryman with winter dress. The spiked helmet, which was the most distinctive element of the Russian infantrymen's dress, was introduced in 1844. It was very similar to the contemporary Prussian *pickelhaube* – which came into use in 1843 – but had been designed one year before the Prussian helmet. This headgear had brass fittings and frontal plate bearing a double-headed Russian Eagle. On campaign and for everyday service, the helmet was replaced with the much more comfortable *furazhka* cap, as worn by the central figure. This had a detachable leather peak for officers and was peakless for other ranks. The jägers or light infantrymen used it much more frequently than the line infantrymen. In winter, a simple single-breasted grey cloth greatcoat was worn by all the foot units.

was made up of one company of grenadiers and three companies of fusiliers, all with 250 men each. The three divisions made up the Grenadier Corps, an elite force consisting of the tallest and strongest infantrymen of the Russian Army which was usually employed only when absolutely necessary (such as in major pitched battles). Differently from the heavy infantry, the line infantry and light infantry were part of the same structure, consisting of six Infantry Corps, numbered 1–6, each of which comprised three divisions (for a total of eighteen infantry divisions, numbered 1–18).

The new uniforms of the Russian infantry introduced in 1855 (from left to right): line infantryman with spiked helmet, drummer with shako and line infantryman with shako. In 1855, the new double-breasted tunic shown here replaced the single-breasted coatee introduced in 1826. The new uniform, however, was adopted very slowly and thus it was used on only a very small scale during the last months of the Crimean War. The dress regulations of 1855 also replaced the spiked helmet with the new black shako shown here; this was never seen during the Crimean War, since most of the regiments continued to wear their old helmets for several months (like the soldier on the left). The shako was quite short-lived and came out of use in 1864. Musicians had distinctive shoulder wings and – with the M1826 coatee – additional stripes of lace on the sleeves.

A division consisted of a 1st Brigade made up of two line infantry regiments and a 2nd Brigade of two light infantry regiments (jägers). As a result, the Russian Army had thirty-six regiments of line infantry and thirty-six regiments of light infantry, all with four battalions each for a total of 288 foot battalions. Each of these battalions had 250 men, with one grenadier company and three musketeer companies for the line infantry or one carabineer company and three jäger companies for the light infantry. Each foot regiment also comprised two depot battalions that could be mobilized in case of war. Line units were numbered 1–36 exactly like the light infantry, so the same progressive number was used by one corps of line infantry and one of light infantry. It should be noted, however, that the foot regiments of the Russian Army were not known by their progressive numbers but by their official denominations; a regiment was usually named after its home region/city or its patron (in most cases a noble). With the outbreak of the Crimean War, a 7th and 8th Battalion were added to each of the existing foot regiments instead of creating new units from scratch. With war mobilization, the regiments of the Grenadier Corps also comprised eight battalions each. Attached to each Infantry Corps were one battalion of rifles, one of sappers and one of the train, each organized on four companies. The jäger regiments of the Russian infantry, differently from the single jäger regiment of the Imperial Guard, were armed with smoothbore percussion muskets exactly like the line infantry regiments. Their muskets were produced in a special lighter version and their uniforms had some peculiar elements, but in practice they fought in close order like the line infantry and were almost impossible to distinguish from them on the battlefield. The 'true' light infantry of the Russian Army were the six battalions of riflemen that were attached to each of the Infantry Corps, since these were trained to explore and skirmish in open order and were equipped with modern rifled carbines. The riflemen were specialist marksmen and were frequently employed to conduct special operations. It should be noted, however, that in each foot battalion (line or jäger) there were two NCOs and twenty-four privates armed with rifled carbines and called *shtutsernye* or riflemen.

Cavalry

In 1854, the Russian Army deployed the largest cavalry forces in the world, with units belonging to four different categories: cuirassiers, dragoons, uhlans and hussars. The cuirassiers consisted of eight regiments with six squadrons each, their main task being to act as shock troops on the battlefield in frontal cavalry charges. They were equipped with metal helmets and cuirasses. There were eight regiments of dragoons with ten squadrons each, which despite not wearing metal cuirasses and having distinctive

Russian NCO of the cuirassiers, with metal helmet and cuirass.

Russian trooper of the cuirassiers, with the cuirass worn over the winter greatcoat.

uniforms performed more or less the same heavy cavalry duties as the cuirassiers. The uhlans or lancers consisted of twenty regiments with eight squadrons each, acting as medium cavalry which could fight in pitched battles or conduct reconnaissance missions. The fourteen regiments of hussars had eight squadrons each, tasked with performing traditional light cavalry duties like scouting and skirmishing. As a result

Russian trooper (left) and officer (right) of the cuirassiers. The figure on the left has the white single-breasted uniform used until 1855, when the new double-breasted tunic worn by the officer on the right was introduced.

Russian trooper of the hussars, with the uniform worn until 1855.

Russian trooper of the hussars, with the new uniform introduced in 1855.

of the above organization, which was introduced in 1833, the Russian regular cavalry deployed a total of fifty regiments with 400 squadrons. The various regiments were assembled as follows into independent Cavalry Corps or were attached to Infantry/Grenadier Corps:

- 1st Reserve Cavalry Corps: one division with four cuirassier regiments and one division with four uhlan regiments.
- 2nd Reserve Cavalry Corps: one division with four cuirassier regiments and one division with four uhlan regiments.
- 3rd Reserve Cavalry Corps: two divisions with four dragoon regiments each.
- Attached to the Grenadier Corps: one light cavalry division with two regiments of uhlans and two regiments of hussars.
- Attached to the I Infantry Corps: one light cavalry division with two regiments of uhlans and two regiments of hussars.
- Attached to the II Infantry Corps: one light cavalry division with two regiments of uhlans and two regiments of hussars.
- Attached to the III Infantry Corps: one light cavalry division with two regiments of uhlans and two regiments of hussars.
- Attached to the IV Infantry Corps: one light cavalry division with two regiments of uhlans and two regiments of hussars.
- Attached to the V Infantry Corps: one light cavalry division with two regiments of uhlans and two regiments of hussars.
- Attached to the VI Infantry Corps: one light cavalry division with two regiments of uhlans and two regiments of hussars.

Each cavalry division consisted of two brigades with two regiments each. The three Reserve Cavalry Corps, comprising the heavily equipped cuirassiers and dragoons, formed a strategic reserve that was employed only during major campaigns. There were 170 men in the squadrons of all regiments. Curiously, the Russian cavalry included two double-squadrons of Mounted Pioneers, which were made up of pioneers who had a higher degree of mobility than their foot equivalents. The Russian mounted troops also contained a Regiment of Gendarmes, acting as mounted military police and organized like a foot battalion.

Artillery and technical corps

The artillery of the Russian Army comprised both foot and horse units, organized similarly to the cavalry, to provide fire support to the Grenadier Corps and the six

Infantry Corps. In 1854, the order of battle of the Russian artillery was as follows, which was the same general structure that had been introduced in 1833:

- Grenadier Artillery Division, attached to the Grenadier Corps: 1st, 2nd and 3rd Grenadier Artillery Brigades, plus 7th Horse Artillery Brigade.
- 1st Artillery Division, attached to the I Infantry Corps: 1st, 2nd and 3rd Foot Artillery Brigades, plus 1st Horse Artillery Brigade.
- 2nd Artillery Division, attached to the II Infantry Corps: 4th, 5th and 6th Foot Artillery Brigades, plus 2nd Horse Artillery Brigade.
- 3rd Artillery Division, attached to the III Infantry Corps: 7th, 8th and 9th Foot Artillery Brigades, plus 3rd Horse Artillery Brigade.
- 4th Artillery Division, attached to the IV Infantry Corps: 10th, 11th and 12th Foot Artillery Brigades, plus 4th Horse Artillery Brigade.
- 5th Artillery Division, attached to the V Infantry Corps: 13th, 14th and 15th Foot Artillery Brigades, plus 5th Horse Artillery Brigade.
- 6th Artillery Division, attached to the VI Infantry Corps: 16th, 17th and 18th Foot Artillery Brigades, plus 6th Horse Artillery Brigade.
- 1st Horse Artillery Division, attached to the 1st Reserve Cavalry Corps: 1st and 2nd Horse Artillery Brigades.
- 2nd Horse Artillery Division, attached to the 2nd Reserve Cavalry Corps: 3rd and 4th Horse Artillery Brigades.
- 3rd Horse Artillery Division, attached to the 3rd Reserve Cavalry Corps: 5th and 6th Horse Artillery Brigades.

In addition to the above there was the independent 19th Foot Artillery Brigade deployed in Finland and a Horse Artillery Reserve consisting of nine mounted batteries. As is clear from the order of battle, the horse artillery was tasked with providing fire support to the three divisions of heavy cavalry. The Grenadier Artillery Brigades consisted of two heavy batteries and three light batteries each. The Foot Artillery Brigades, meanwhile, had different internal establishments: the 1st, 4th, 7th, 10th, 13th and 16th had two heavy batteries and two light batteries, whereas the remaining ones had one heavy battery and three light batteries. The Horse Artillery Brigades had two light batteries each. The Horse Artillery Divisions were not structured on brigades and each of them comprised two heavy batteries and four light batteries. The batteries of the foot artillery had twelve guns each: six 12-pdr and six 18-pdr cannons for the heavy batteries, and eight 6-pdr and four 9-pdr cannons for the light batteries. The batteries of the horse artillery and the grenadier artillery had eight guns each: eight 18-pdr cannons for the heavy batteries, and four

Russian gunners of the Imperial Guard's foot artillery (left) and the regular foot artillery (right). Black was the distinctive colour of the Russian artillery, as it was in the armies of many other European countries. The foot artillery was dressed very similarly to the line infantry.

The Russian Army 147

Russian gunner of the horse artillery, with M1855 double-breasted tunic.

6-pdr and four 9-pdr cannons for the light batteries. Foot and horse batteries all had the same internal composition: one lieutenant-colonel, one captain, one staff captain, two lieutenants, two second-lieutenants, one sergeant-major, twenty-three sergeants, six musicians, sixty-eight bombardiers and 176 gunners. The sappers of the Russian Army consisted of seven battalions with four companies each; a single sapper company had 250 men. Each battalion was attached to the six Infantry Corps or to the Grenadier Corps. There were also two autonomous Reserve Sapper Battalions, each of which comprised one sapper company and three pontoon companies. Each of the six pontoon companies, in case of war mobilization, was assigned to one of the Infantry Corps. The train was organized on ten brigades with a variable number of battalions; each of these brigades was attached to one of the Grenadier, Infantry or Reserve Cavalry Corps. The number of battalions in each Train Brigade corresponded to the number of divisions that were included into the Army Corps to which the Train Brigade was attached. The Train Brigade of each Army Corps consisted of the latter's non-combatant soldiers who made up the depot units. The Horse Artillery Reserve had its own autonomous half-brigade of train.

Reserve Army

The Russian Army contained some very large reserve forces, which were independent from the Regular Army but had a quite precise organization. Each regular unit maintained permanent peacetime cadres that were to make up the Reserve, or *Rezervnye*. Each foot regiment of the Imperial Guard had one reserve battalion, while each regiment of the Grenadier Corps and Infantry Corps had two reserve battalions. These had different functions: to act as the proper reserve and to be a replacement battalion to replenish the losses of its parent unit. With the mobilization that followed the outbreak of the Crimean War, the Reserve Army was greatly enlarged and each foot regiment of the Imperial Guard formed three reserve battalions. These were assembled into twelve temporary regiments, which were organized as three Guard Reserve Divisions with four regiments each. Each foot regiment of the Grenadier Corps and the Infantry Corps activated two reserve battalions and two replacement battalions. The reserve and replacement battalions of each infantry division were brought together to form Reserve Brigades and Replacement Brigades, each with two regiments. Each Reserve Regiment or Replacement Regiment consisted of four battalions. The rifle battalions attached to each Infantry Corps were also much expanded, gradually forming three reserve battalions and two replacement battalions each. The sapper battalions of the Imperial Guard and Grenadier Corps each formed one reserve half-battalion, while those attached to the Infantry Corps formed a whole reserve battalion each. In peacetime, each cavalry regiment had one reserve squadron, but upon mobilization for war each unit was required to raise one replacement squadron (the dragoon regiments were an exception to this rule, since they had two reserve squadrons and one replacement squadron). The reserve squadrons and replacement squadrons from the mounted units of the Imperial Guard and Grenadier Corps created an autonomous Guard Cavalry Corps that consisted of seven regiments with four squadrons each. The reserve squadrons and replacement squadrons of each heavy cavalry division were assembled together to form a Reserve Heavy Cavalry Brigade. The reserve squadrons and replacement squadrons of the light cavalry regiments attached to the Infantry Corps were combined to form a Reserve Light Cavalry Division that consisted of four composite regiments. Each of the latter comprised three squadrons of uhlans and three squadrons of hussars. In peacetime, the foot artillery of the Imperial Guard and the Grenadier Corps had three reserve batteries and three replacement batteries each. The six artillery divisions attached to the Infantry Corps each had three reserve batteries and three replacement batteries, while the horse artillery brigades attached to the Infantry Corps had one reserve battery each. Following the outbreak of the Crimean War, a Reserve Artillery Brigade with three batteries was organized for each foot artillery brigade and horse artillery brigade.

The Russian military could thus count on a 'second-line army' thanks to the many reserve units. These were formed by recalling soldiers of the lower ranks who were on indefinite leave. According to Russian military law, the length of service for privates and NCOs was set at twenty-five years for the Regular Army and twenty-two years for the Imperial Guard. Upon reaching fifteen years of service without having committed faults, however, a soldier was allowed to leave the ranks of his unit. The men released on indefinite leave after serving for fifteen years were required to muster every year for a month-long training session. Those released on indefinite leave after serving for twenty-five or twenty-two years were not obliged to train annually after leaving the army. This system had been introduced in 1834 but never worked particularly well, because many soldiers died soon after leaving active service and thus were no longer available to make up the reserve forces. The living conditions of the privates were extremely harsh and it was very rare for a soldier to have a long life. To fill the gaps in the reserve and replacement corps during the Crimean War, the Russian authorities had no choice but to call for new recruits through conscription. The drafted men had to leave their families and serve with the army until the end of hostilities.

Interior Forces

Russia's interior forces comprised a variety of units, which had diverse combat capabilities and were tasked with performing specific tasks. In general, however, they were all intended to prevent the outbreak of internal rebellions and worked as auxiliaries of the regular Russian Army. There were three autonomous infantry divisions that were deployed in strategically important areas of the Russian Empire: the 22nd Finnish Division, 23rd Orenburg Division and 24th Siberia Division. These were organized like normal divisions of the Russian Army, but were collectively known as 'Frontier Forces'. The 22nd Division garrisoned the semi-autonomous Grand Duchy of Finland, which had a long border with the Kingdom of Sweden and Norway and was quite isolated from the rest of the Russian Empire (despite being quite near to the imperial capital of St Petersburg). The 23rd Division garrisoned the Russian entrance to Central Asia – the area surrounding Orenburg north of present-day Kazakhstan. The 24th Division had one of the most difficult tasks of the entire Russian Army, having to garrison the enormous territory of Siberia that stretched from the Ural Mountains in the east to Alaska in the west. The Siberia Division, created in 1829, comprised sixteen battalions of line infantry that were grouped into three brigades. These units were mostly tasked with garrisoning the line of fortified posts that marked the border between Russian Siberia and the lands of the Chinese Qing Empire (which included Mongolia). The line infantry battalions of the Siberia Division also had to patrol Russian Alaska, but until the outbreak of the Crimean War none of them was ever sent to North America. When hostilities with Britain commenced, the Russians feared that the British could attack their outposts in Alaska from their territorial possessions in Canada or from the bases of the Hudson's Bay Company. Consequently, a composite line infantry battalion with four companies taken from three different battalions of the Siberia Division was formed and sent to the Pacific coastline of Siberia. From here, 200 men of the unit were sent to Sitka, the main Russian base in Alaska. These were the first regular Russian soldiers to serve in Russian America since the early nineteenth century, when the Russians had consolidated their position in Alaska by fighting against local native tribes. The new garrison of Russian America was never attacked by the British, but had to fight some skirmishes with native populations. The Finnish Division consisted of twelve line infantry battalions and was mobilized during the Crimean War to face British naval attacks against Russian positions in the Baltic, while the Orenburg Division had ten line infantry battalions that continued to perform their usual duties during the conflict.

The bulk of the Russian interior forces were represented by fifty independent line infantry battalions which garrisoned the most important cities and fortresses of European Russia. These battalions were assembled into nine military regions from 1845, and each of them consisted of four companies. The garrison battalions were supported by ninety-eight garrison artillery companies and 105 companies of invalids. The garrison artillery companies manned the many batteries that were scattered across the fortresses of the Russian Empire, while the companies of invalids were made up of veteran soldiers who were no longer fit for active service but could perform static defensive duties. The garrison artillery companies had a standard establishment of four officers and 165 men. The interior forces also included an Engineer Command that consisted of 352 detached officers who were tasked with directing and supervising the construction and repair of military fortifications and installations scattered across Russia. The Engineer Command could count on a labour force made up of twenty-six workers' companies and fifty-two penal companies. The first of these comprised military workers, while the second consisted of ex-deserters or former soldiers who had committed crimes while in the army. The workers' companies had a standard establishment of three officers and 208 privates, while the penal companies did not have a fixed establishment. Both acted under the orders of the Engineer Command and could also be employed to construct civil infrastructure such as roads or bridges. A Corps of Topographers was completely autonomous from the Engineer Command, being structured on nine companies and having as its main task drawing accurate maps representing the immense territory of Russia.

The Army of the Caucasus

As already mentioned, Russia was involved for most of the nineteenth century in a bloody and difficult conflict in the Caucasus, with the local populations strongly opposing penetration by Russian forces. Warfare in the Caucasus was brutal and rapid: the tribal communities living in the high mountains of the region were effective at employing skirmishing tactics, aided by their deep knowledge of their homeland. The Caucasian fighters used hit-and-run tactics to slow down the superior Russian forces and were masters in organizing ambushes. Their resistance lasted for many years, during which the Russians suffered several unexpected defeats. The Russian soldiers were not used to guerrilla warfare and suffered greatly from the weather conditions that were typical of the Caucasus, characterized by hot temperatures during the day and freezing cold at night. As a result of the hard lessons learned during their first years of campaigning in the Caucasus, the Russians decided to create a separate branch within their armed forces known as the Army of the Caucasus. This was composed of the Russian formations that had already been serving in the Caucasus for several years, whose soldiers had gained a lot of precious experience in combat

Russian infantrymen of the Army of the Caucasus. This army, since 1848, had its own autonomous dress regulations. The figure on the left wears the M1848 uniform, which included a modern single-breasted tunic that was never adopted by the rest of the Russian Army. The figure on the right wears the new M1855 uniform, with the same double-breasted tunic used by the rest of the Russian Army. The headgear of both soldiers is the Caucasian *papacha* covered with fur that was introduced in 1848.

against the local mountain fighters. In 1801, the Russians had the following military units in the Caucasus: twenty-five line infantry battalions, twenty dragoon squadrons and five field artillery batteries. In 1811, these were brought together to form two independent infantry divisions, the 19th and the 20th. In 1815, these received the new official denomination of the Separate Georgian Corps, which can be considered an ancestor of the Army of the Caucasus. In 1816, the Georgian Corps was expanded with the addition of a Reserve Grenadier Brigade, which consisted of two

Russian officer of the Nijegorodskii Dragoon Regiment, which made up the regular cavalry of the Army of the Caucasus. According to the latter's dress regulations of 1848, the Nijegorodskii Dragoons were the only regular cavalry to wear the Caucasian-style uniform shown here. This comprised a curious helmet covered with fur and a single-breasted kaftan with *gazyrs* breast pockets.

grenadier regiments and an artillery brigade with four batteries. The Reserve Grenadier Brigade was created as an elite shock force, and in practice was the Caucasian detachment of the larger Grenadier Corps. In August 1820, the Separate Georgian Corps changed its name and started to be known as Army of the Caucasus. In 1845, following an escalation in the military operations fought in the Caucasus, a third infantry division was added to the Army of the Caucasus. This, the 21st, had the same internal structure as the other infantry divisions of the Russian Army (including the two that were already part of the Army of the Caucasus). Each infantry division had its own divisional artillery. Meanwhile, the cavalry of the Army of the Caucasus consisted of the Nijegorodskii Dragoon Regiment's ten squadrons. The mountainous terrain of the Caucasus was not well suited for cavalry actions, so the Russians deployed only this single regular mounted regiment on that front. On 17 April 1854, the Reserve Grenadier Brigade was expanded and transformed into the Grenadier Division of the Caucasus, with two brigades of two grenadier regiments each, plus one brigade of artillery. As a result, during the Crimean War, the Army of the Caucasus mustered one division of grenadiers and three divisions of line infantry.

The Russians also had a number of garrison line infantry battalions in the Causasus, which were assembled into three separate organizations according to their distribution around the territory: the Black Sea Battalions, Caucasus Battalions and Georgian Battalions. There were sixteen Black Sea Battalions, thirteen Caucasus Battalions and eighteen Georgian Battalions, all of which had four companies apiece. The Army of the Caucasus also comprised several units of irregulars, which were recruited locally from supporters of the Russian cause or from those areas of the Caucasus that had already been occupied by the Russian Army. These formations, which were particularly effective despite not being always well disciplined, will be covered in the following section dedicated to the irregular contingents of the Russian military.

Irregular Forces and Militia

The immense population of the Russian Empire included several peoples with a tribal social organization living in areas that were geographically isolated. These ethnic minorities, which could be quite numerous and nomadic, mostly consisted of Cossacks who had settled on the frontier areas of the Russian Empire, but there also were those from the Caucasus or Central Asia with their own peculiar political structures. During the Napoleonic Wars, due to the emergency caused by the French invasion of 1812, the Russian authorities had been obliged to raise substantial numbers of soldiers from these communities, and their combat experience from 1812–14 showed that these tribal fighters from distant corners of the empire had a great military potential (especially if employed as light cavalry). As a result, after the end of the Napoleonic Wars, the Russian military tried to give a much more stable organization to their irregular forces. These were structured on regional 'hosts', or 'armies', which were quite autonomous from the centralized Russian Army. Each host was stationed in a particular area of the empire and its units could be employed away from their homeland only in the event of a military emergency (such as a foreign invasion of Russian territory). By 1854, the irregular forces of the Russian Army were organized into eleven semi-independent regional armies: the Don Host, Black Sea Host, Caucasian Host, Ural Host, Astrakhan Host, Danube Host, Orenburg Host, Azov Host, Siberian Host, Transbaikal Host and Bashkir Host. The Don Host, whose home territory was between south-eastern Ukraine and the north-western Caucasus, was the most powerful of these formations. It deployed fifty-four regiments of Cossacks, nine batteries of mounted artillery and one company of workers, with each regiment of light cavalry – like for all the mounted units of the irregular forces – consisting of six '*sotnias*', or 'hundreds' (the irregular cavalry was not structured on squadrons but on hundreds/companies). The Black Sea Host's home territory was centred around the Kuban River in the north-western Caucasus, and it deployed twelve regiments of Cossacks, nine battalions of infantry and one company of workers. The Caucasian Host, which was directly involved in operations fought in its home region, mustered eighteen regiments of Cossacks and two battalions of infantry. The Ural Host, whose homeland was the Ural Mountains that marked the border between European and Asiatic Russia, deployed three regiments of Cossacks.

The Astrakhan Host, settled north-east of the Caucasus on the borders with present-day Kazakhstan, consisted of three regiments of Cossacks. The Danube Host was the last one to be formed, being established only in 1828 as a consequence of the ongoing conflict between Russia and the Ottoman Empire. In 1775, following the dissolution of their state, several Zaporozhian Cossacks had moved into the lands of the Ottoman Empire and settled around the mouth of the Danube. From 1806, these political refugees started to be involved in the military campaigns that were fought along the Danube between the Russians and the Turks, deciding to side with the former. In 1828, the Danube Cossacks were organized as a host and in 1829 their homeland was ceded by the Ottomans to the Russians. By 1854 there were two

Trooper (left) and officer (right) of the Don Cossacks. These wore dark blue uniforms with red facings and their general appearance was much more 'regular' than that of the other Cossack contingents. The *papacha* was the standard headgear of all the Cossack hosts.

Trooper of the Caucasian Cossacks (left) and Bashkir mounted warrior (right). The latter is dressed more or less like one of Genghis Khan's Mongols and is armed with a composite bow.

regiments of Danube Cossacks, tasked with guarding the military frontier located near the mouth of the great river.

The Orenburg Host, whose homeland was centred around the city of Orenburg on the northern border of Kazakhstan, deployed six battalions of mounted Cossacks, while the Azov Host, with a home territory located to the east of Crimea on the coastline of the Azov Sea, consisted of a single Cossack regiment that was disbanded in 1856. The Siberian Host, with a homeland in the western portion of Siberia, had contributed decisively to the early Russian colonization of Siberia. By 1854, it mustered ten regiments of Cossacks. The Transbaikal Host, whose homeland corresponded to the eastern portion of Siberia, was mostly tasked with guarding the frontier with the Chinese Empire, stretching from Mongolia to Manchuria. It deployed a sizeable military force of six mounted regiments and twelve foot battalions. The Bashkir Host was one of the last to adopt some form of proper organization, its soldiers only being given uniforms in 1829. The Bashkirs lived in the Russian lands bordering with northern Kazakhstan, and their lifestyle had changed very little since the days of Genghis Khan. During the Napoleonic Wars, wearing chainmail and being armed with composite bows, they impressed the French even more than did the Cossacks. In 1854, the Bashkir Host consisted of five cavalry regiments, but its establishment was progressively expanded with the addition of four mounted regiments of Tatars (which had until then been organized as a separate host). In addition to the units of the various hosts, there were also three independent regiments of Cossacks recruited from the communities of Little Russia (a region of eastern Ukraine which still today is inhabited by many Russians). Irregular forces could thus provide some impressive cavalry contingents to the Russian military, with not all the hosts being made up of Cossacks, since communities such as the Bashkirs were completely independent from them. However, all the hosts provided the Russians with excellent light cavalry. They may sometimes have been criticized by their Russian commanders because they lacked discipline and were equipped with old-fashioned weapons, but the Cossacks and the other irregular horsemen were the best light cavalry in the world at conducting scouting or skirmishing operations.

The irregular forces of the Russian Army also comprised several autonomous corps that had their own unique history. In the Caucasus, for example, the Russians could count on the support of the Georgians, who had been oppressed as a people for centuries since they were Christians in a region inhabited by a majority of Muslims. The Georgians had supported the Russians since the early years of their campaigns in the Caucasus. The Russian government trusted them implicitly, and in 1832 some Georgian militiamen were permitted to form a single regiment of infantry with four *sotnias* (hundreds). In 1849, another foot unit of Georgians, again with four *sotnias*, was formed from chosen militia, then an independent *sotnia* of Georgians was created in 1851 to guard the border with the Ottoman Empire around Ozurget. Some units of the irregular forces were part of the Army of the Caucasus and made a significant contribution to its war effort. On 2 June 1835, Russian military authorities in the Caucasus decided to form two new corps that were recruited on a local basis: the Muslim Irregular Horse Regiment and Caucasian Mountaineer Irregular Horse Regiment, both consisting of six *sotnias*. The Muslim Irregular Horse Regiment was made up of Muslims who had already shown their loyalty towards Russia, most of whom came from present-day Azerbaijan; it fought very well on several occasions, to the point that the Circassians of the Imperial Guard were recruited from its ranks. The Caucasian Mountaineer Irregular Horse Regiment comprised Caucasian mountainmen (notably Chechens) and fought with the same methods as its enemies. In 1842, the Russians also recruited 200 irregular light cavalry from Daghestan, who ten years later were expanded to six *sotnias* and were consolidated into a unit known as the Daghestan Irregular Horse Regiment.

In the event of a military emergency, the Russian government could potentially mobilize all able-bodied male subjects of the empire and assemble them to form the People's Militia, or Narodnoe Opolcheniye. This formation did not have a stable organization, since it was mobilized only in case of need. Its numbers could vary

Russian militiamen of the Narodnoe Opolcheniye, wearing the traditional grey peaked caps and kaftans of their corps. The badge of the militia, a Maltese cross, is visible on the front of the headgear.

greatly, and it usually consisted only of militia from the rural areas of European Russia (where millions of poor peasants lived in a state of misery under the control of a few landowners). The first large-scale mobilization of the People's Militia took place in 1812 when Russia was invaded by Napoleon; a total of 300,000 militia were armed and sent to the front, where they sometimes performed quite well against the French invaders. These improvised soldiers had no discipline and uniforms to speak of, but their level of patriotism was extremely high. The second large-scale mobilization took place during the Crimean War, when 245,000 militia were prepared for combat service. These were all armed with old flintlock muskets dating back to the Napoleonic Wars and had never seen the battlefield before. They were assembled into 236 infantry companies, forty-five of which went to Crimea and participated – with auxiliary roles – in combat operations. On 25 October 1854, by bringing together the best militiamen from the peasant communities on the Romanov family's estates, a special regiment of the Narodnoe Opolcheniye was formed. This was temporarily attached to the Imperial Guard before being disbanded at the end of the war in 1856.

Naval and foreign units

The Russian Navy of 1854 was one of the largest in the world and had a remarkable level of combat experience. It consisted of five independent divisions, which were assembled into two fleets: the Baltic Fleet having three divisions and the Black Sea Fleet two divisions. Since the days of Peter the Great, the Russian Navy had comprised a strong and efficient Naval Infantry Corps, but this was disbanded in 1813 and its members were used to replenish army losses. As a result, by 1854, it was sailors who performed the naval infantry and naval artillery duties that had been previously assigned to marines. Each division of the Russian Navy was structured on three brigades, each of which comprised three '*ekipazhi*', or 'crews'. The Baltic Fleet had twenty-seven *ekipazhi*, while the Black Sea Fleet had eighteen. In addition, there were two small and autonomous flotillas (one on the Caspian Sea and another on the Pacific coast of Kamchatka) that had a single crew each. A single *ekipazh* consisted of the following elements: one first-captain, one second-captain, four captain-lieutenants, twelve lieutenants, twelve ensigns, eighty NCOs, twenty-five musicians and 1,000 sailors. Each crew was structured on four companies of 250 sailors, and attached to it was a fifth company consisting of 100 non-combatants. The various *ekipazhi* were divided among several ships, providing them with the necessary number of sailors as well as naval infantrymen and artillerymen. Each of the units included a few men who were trained as sharpshooters. The Russian Navy also comprised some non-combatant crews, whose members acted as naval workers to repair and build ships or ports. In the spring of 1854, following the outbreak of the Crimean War, the Russians realized they needed some proper marines and created two Temporary Naval Landing Battalions. These were structured on six platoons with forty-eight men each, and their members were chosen from the sharpshooters of the best *ekipazhi*. In July 1854, another two temporary battalions of marines were established, followed by another three in September.

Although the Russians had no allies during the Crimean War, they could count on the support of Greece. During the Russo-Turkish War of 1768–74, the Russian Navy had entered the Aegean Sea to support the first national uprising by the Greeks against the Ottomans. A little later, during the Napoleonic Wars, the Russians continued to help the Greek patriots by providing them with diplomatic support and weapons. When the Greek War of Independence began in 1821, Russia sided with the Greeks and its fleet destroyed an Ottoman naval force during the decisive Battle of Navarino. In 1828 and 1829, to help seal Greek independence, a Russian army attacked Ottoman positions in the Balkans. When Greece officially became an independent country in 1830, it was thus mostly thanks to Russian support. The Russians had been pursuing a clear policy to create a friendly Christian state in the southern Balkans that could help them conquer Constantinople and thereby gain direct access to the Mediterranean. As a result of the excellent relations between the Greeks and Russians, many young Greek aristocrats and future patriots had since 1770 gone to study in Russian military institutions, helping strengthen the links between the two countries. During the Russo-Turkish War, the Russians raised eight battalions of infantry from the Greek insurgents and embarked them on their warships operating in the Aegean. When the conflict ended, however, most of the Greek soldiers in Russian service could not return to their homeland because the national uprising had been crushed by the Turks, who were perpetrating massacres in Greece. Together with other political refugees, they decided to leave Greece after 1774 and were settled in Crimea by the Russians. The Crimean peninsula, ceded to Russia by the Ottomans following the war of 1768–74, had been inhabited by a numerous and prosperous Greek minority since Antiquity. Consequently, Crimea became a base from 1775 for all future operations by the Greek patriots. In 1775, in order to create a reliable local military force that could defend Crimea from incursions by the Ottomans and from revolts by the local Tatars, the Russians raised a light infantry regiment with twenty companies from the Greek communities of the region. The main base of the new unit was Balaclava and each of the Greek soldiers was given a grant of land in exchange for their military service. The Greek unit was part of the Russian Army's irregular forces, but some of its companies were frequently embarked on the warships of the Russian Navy to act as naval infantry in combat

Officer (right) and soldiers (left) of the Balaclava Greek Infantry Battalion. The uniform of this irregular corps was very distinctive: black helmet with yellow crest and brass fittings, black single-breasted jacket with red collar and pointed cuffs piped in yellow, red frontal plastron with yellow piping and brass buttons, red waist-sash, red loose trousers and black leather boots.

against the Turks. In 1797, the Greek corps was reduced to just three companies and received the new denomination of the Balaclava Greek Infantry Battalion, which had the privilege of acting as the Tsar's personal guard when he visited Crimea. During the Crimean War, the unit defended Balaclava from British attacks with enormous courage before being almost annihilated. The Balaclava Greek Infantry Battalion was officially disbanded in 1859.

When the Crimean War broke out, the Kingdom of Greece was forced to remain neutral due to the strong commercial links it had with Britain and France. However, both its government and population were strongly pro-Russian. In consequence, hundreds of Greek volunteers from every corner of the Balkans went to the Danubian Principalities to join the ranks of the Russian armed forces. These men were assembled into a volunteer light infantry battalion with four companies in December 1853, but it was soon expanded thanks to the arrival of fresh volunteers and then comprised

Contemporary painting showing the outfit of the Greek Legion. The general appearance of the volunteers, who wore no proper uniform, was very similar to that of the contemporary Evzones (light infantry) of the Greek Army: red *farion* cap with silk tassel, *fermeli* waistcoat decorated with rich embroiderings, white *ypodetes* wide-sleeved shirt, white *foustanella* pleated skirt, *periskelides* woollen stockings and *tsarouicha* mountain shoes.

six four-company battalions. The first two battalions were made up of Greeks, another two consisted of Christian volunteers from various parts of the Balkans and the remaining two comprised volunteers from the Danubian Principalities of Moldavia and Wallachia. After the Russians were forced to abandon the Danubian Principalities, all the battalions of volunteers were disbanded, but most of the Greeks refused to go back home. Instead, they were reorganized on six companies as a single light infantry battalion. They were sent to Crimea, where they were promised a land grant at the end of hostilities, making them military settlers like the soldiers of the Balaclava Greek Infantry Battalion. The Greek volunteers, by now known as the Greek Legion, fought with great valour during the bloody siege of Sevastopol, and in 1855 the Tsar decided to change the name of their battalion to the Greek Legion of Emperor Nicholas I. While the Greeks generally resented military discipline, were armed with old flintlocks and were dressed with the traditional costume of the Hellenic mountaineers, they were extremely efficient in combat. What remained of the Greek Legion was disbanded in 1856, after which only a few of its members became settlers in Crimea.

Chapter 4

The Ottoman Army

The army of 1826–39

By the time of the Napoleonic Wars, the Ottoman armed forces – after more than a century of slow decline – consisted of five main categories of troops: the salaried and professional *kapikulu* or regulars, the semi-professional *toprakh* regional contingents, the local militias of the *miri-askeris* (available for use during short campaigns), the *yerli nerefats* or general militias of the urban centres and the *gonulluyan* or general militias of the countryside. The core of the regular *kapikulu* forces were the famous Janissaries, who had previously been an excellent fighting corps but had gradually (especially during the eighteenth century) become a corrupt hereditary warrior caste that enjoyed a series of privileges. The Janissaries were organized into regiments and underwent some regular military training, but in practice they had very little combat capability, their units lacking discipline and their officers – who obtained their ranks through purchase rather than ability – were more interested in politics than improving the standards of service of their men. Every able-bodied free man who was a friend or relative of an officer could now join the ranks of the Janissaries without undergoing any form of selection. It was just as easy to leave the *kapikulu* regulars, with every soldier able to resign when he wanted. As a result of this situation, each *orta* or regiment of Janissaries had a very flexible structure, with the number of its components varying widely. Several of the senior Janissaries became rich enough to have their own personal servants and to pay them to perform their military duties. These auxiliaries, known as *yamaks*, became increasingly numerous and were gradually transformed into proper mercenaries.

The Ottoman cavalry consisted of three categories of troops: the feudal cavalry of the Timarli Sipahis, the salaried cavalry of the Kapikulu Sipahis and the Delis irregular cavalry. The Timarli Sipahis were the last remnants of the Ottomans' medieval military organization and consisted of individuals who had been given land and property in the provinces in exchange for serving as cavalry. These 'Provincial Sipahis' acted as imperial officials to collect taxes and formed an elite social class, but over time they lost most of their military importance due to the rise of the Kapikulu Sipahis. The latter were paid on a regular basis by the central government, making them the cavalry equivalent of the Janissaries. They were organized into six divisions, each of which performed specific duties and had peculiar weaponry. The Delis were irregulars recruited by the Ottomans from the warlike communities living on the borders of their empire, mostly in the Balkans. They were employed as highly mobile scouts and skirmishers, and were capable of conducting long-range reconnaissance missions as well as devastating incursions. From 1770, the Ottomans started to realize they needed a general modernization of their military forces; what they absolutely needed was a new body of effective line infantry to replace the old-fashioned Janissaries and a well-organized artillery that could face the European armies on almost equal terms. But the Janissaries, as well as the Sipahis, were extremely jealous of their privileges and were opposed to any project of reform. Their traditionalist officers never accepted the need to introduce strict discipline in their units or to replace their men's antiquated matchlock muskets with European flintlocks. Mahmud II became the Sultan of the Ottoman Empire in 1808 after two bloody military coups organized by the Janissaries aimed at stopping any attempted military reform. To gain power and retain it, the new Turkish monarch had no choice but to form a political alliance with the most conservative elements of his armed forces. However, it slowly became apparent that the military situation of the Ottoman Empire was no longer sustainable. Around 1825, Mahmud II realized that a general reform of his armed forces was vital and he finally decided to eliminate the Janissaries before launching a general reform of the army.

The Janissaries had originally been recruited according to a system known as *devsirme*, based on child slavery; young Christian boys, mostly from the Balkan lands of the Ottoman Empire that were collectively known as Rumelia, were methodically enslaved and converted to Islam in order to be incorporated into the ranks of the Janissaries and thus become part of the Ottoman Army. By the beginning of the nineteenth century, however, the original enslaved boys from Christian families had been replaced with Turkish youths who wanted to become Janissaries merely to enjoy their privileges. Mahmud II, determined to reduce the political power of his professional foot soldiers, formed an alliance with the long-standing rivals of the Janissaries, the cavalry Sipahis, who hoped that the dissolution of the Janissaries would transform them into the most important military force of the Ottoman Empire. In early 1826, the Sultan informed the Janissaries that he was going to organize a new army structured and trained along modern European lines. The Janissaries, as predicted by Mahmud II, mutinied and advanced on the Sultan's palace to depose him. Mahmud II, however, had prepared an effective response with the help of the Sipahis. During harsh street fighting in Constantinople, more than 4,000 Janissaries were killed, the survivors fleeing from the Ottoman capital or being captured. Mahmud II officially disbanded the Janissaries as a military institution and confiscated all their possessions. By the end of 1826, all the captured Janissaries had been executed, meaning the demise of the most important component of the 'traditional' Ottoman Army. The destruction of the Janissaries, commonly known as the 'Auspicious Incident' since it was well planned by Mahmud II, marked a turning point in the history of the Ottoman Empire. Soon after these events, the Sipahis increased their political power, but this did not last for long: in 1828, shortly after having organized his new westernized army, the Sultan revoked their privileges and dismissed them. Being in no condition to fight against the superior forces of the government, the Sipahis retired honourably and peacefully without causing bloodshed. Their older members were allowed by the Sultan to hang up their weapons and keep their land and properties until their death. Most of the younger Sipahis, however, joined the ranks of Mahmud II's new army. These were initially known as the Asakir-i Mansure-i Muhammediye, or 'The Victorious Soldiers of Muhammad', because they had defeated the Janissaries, but the reformed Ottoman Army soon assumed the simpler denomination of the Nizam-i-Cedit, or New Army.

Mahmud II, in his general reform of the Turkish armed forces, could count on a large number of European veterans who had fought in the Napoleonic Wars and were now wandering across the Mediterranean in search of a new military employment. These professional instructors formed the backbone of the new Ottoman units and achieved significant results in just a few years. First of all, in 1826, the Sultan reorganized his Imperial Guard that had practically ceased to exist with the disbandment of the Janissaries. Until the 'Auspicious Incident', the core of the Ottoman Imperial Guard had been the Bostanci, an elite military corps that was attached to the Janissaries. The Bostanci, numbering 600 men at the beginning of the nineteenth century, were responsible for protecting the Sultan's palace and guarding the imperial harem, as well as for rowing the Sultan's barge. They enjoyed even more privileges than the ordinary Janissaries and their chief had the same rank as a pasha. Since they were of no real military use but represented a serious threat to the life of the Sultan, Mahmud II disbanded them and reorganized his Imperial Guard on two regiments of infantry. These were known as Bostansyan-i Hassa, or 'Trained Imperial Bostanci', to differentiate them from the previous traditional guardsmen. The two regiments each consisted of three battalions, and each battalion comprised 900 men assembled into nine companies. Until 1828, the cavalry of the Imperial Guard continued to be provided by the Sipahis, but when they were disbanded a single cavalry regiment of the Imperial Guard was created by using the most loyal of the younger Sipahis. This new unit, equipped with lances, consisted of three squadrons with 150 men each.

The first branch of the Ottoman line army to be reformed after 1826 was the infantry. According to Mahmud II's plans, it would now consist of *tertebs*, or regiments, each of which had fifteen *safs* (companies). Command of a regiment was given to a bimbashee (major) and a single company would have consisted of the following elements: one youzbashee (captain), two moulazeems (lieutenants), one sanjaqdar (flag-bearer), one tchaoosh (sergeant), ten onbashees (corporals) and eighty-five rankers. Each of the new infantry companies had a single small-calibre field gun and a small artillery detachment, the members of which were known as 'cannon infantry' and consisted of one cannon master (officer), eight artillerymen, five cannon wagoners and six orderlies. Initially, just eight of the modern regiments were raised, under the overall command of a single superior officer known as a *bash-bimbashee*, and all their artillery detachments led by a *topchee-bashee*. In 1828, the Ottoman leadership decided to change the organization of their new regular infantry. This was now to consist of regiments known as *alays*, each of which was to be commanded by a colonel (*miralay*). A foot regiment was structured on three battalions or *tabours*, each of which consisted of three companies with 100 men each. Each battalion was commanded by a *bimbashee* and the staff of a regiment comprised one colonel, one lieutenant-colonel and one intendant. The staff of a battalion consisted of one major, two adjutant-majors, one flag-bearer and one secretary. A single company comprised one *youzbashee*, two lieutenants, one sergeant-major, four senior sergeants and one junior sergeant. The detachments of cannon infantry of each regiment were assembled together to form a single company, mustering a total of 120 men and serving a battery of ten field guns. By the outbreak of hostilities with Russia in 1828, the Nizam-i-Cedit comprised a total of thirty-three line infantry regiments, which in theory could be assembled into brigades (*liwas*) that could in turn make up divisions (*hassas*).

Between 1826 and 1828, the cavalry and artillery of the New Army were also reorganized, although both these components remained quite limited numerically. The first cavalry unit of the Nizam-i-Cedit to be formed was the Silistra Cavalry Regiment, a lancer corps that was raised in 1826 in the area surrounding the Danube Delta from the local Christian communities of Zaporozhian Cossacks. The regiment – strangely for a mounted corps – was structured on two battalions, the first of which was entirely equipped with lances and consisted of Cossacks. Soon after this first unit, another two regiments of dragoons (armed with flintlock carbines) were raised, structured on six squadrons with 150 troopers each. By 1828, the same internal organization had been adopted by the Silistra Cavalry Regiment, which assumed the new denomination of the Sesiasker Cavalry Regiment. Meanwhile, the Ottoman artillery was reorganized by Mahmud II on fifty foot batteries and eight mounted batteries, each of which consisted of 100 men and corresponded to a company. The foot batteries were equipped with 6-pdr, 8-pdr and 12-pdr guns, but could also have heavier 24-pdr siege guns that were drawn by buffaloes. The horse batteries and cannon infantry were equipped with light 3-pdr guns. No regiments or battalions of artillery existed, but there was one Regiment of Bombardiers and one Regiment of Miners, each with 1,250 men. The Regiment of Bombardiers (*Humbaraci Ocagi*) was tasked with manufacturing, transporting and firing mortars as well as mines and grenades, playing a very important role during siege operations. In 1828 and 1829 it included a sizeable number of Polish soldiers who had left their country to fight against the Russians. The Regiment of Miners was a unit of combat engineers, whose members acted as sappers.

The New Army of Mahmud II was still completing its organization when a new war with Russia began in 1828. At the time it numbered a total of 35,000 soldiers, but still lacked combat experience. The Nizam-i-Cedit was practically wiped out by the Russians during 1828 and 1829, so after the end of this disastrous conflict the Ottomans had to rebuild their modernized military forces from scratch.

Between 1829 and 1834, the whole Ottoman Army was reorganized. By the end of this difficult process, it consisted of the following units: six regiments of Guard infantry, twenty regiments of line infantry, twenty battalions of provincial infantry, three regiments of Guard cavalry, two regiments of line cavalry and one artillery corps. Apparently, the four new regiments of Guard infantry were formed from the survivors of the pre-1828 New Army's foot regiments, while the twenty regiments of line infantry were brand new units. The twenty battalions of provincial infantry were the first embryonic form of a reserve army and were mostly recruited from the militiamen of Thrace and western Anatolia. The pre-1828 three squadrons of Guard cavalry were transformed into regiments, while the Sesiasker Cavalry Regiment was disbanded after the area around the Danube Delta was ceded to Russia in 1829. As a result, the two remaining regiments of line cavalry were dragoons. The artillery consisted of a variable number of independent companies, with the regiments of bombardiers and miners both disbanded. In 1834, after having restructured his military, the Sultan created a new Military Academy to train the officers of the Nizam-i-Cedit alongside the two engineering schools that had existed since the end of the previous century. In 1836, the provincial units of the Ottoman Army were organized for the first time as the Redeef, or Army Reserve. By 1837, the Nizam-i-Cedit had seen further expansion and comprised the following units: two regiments of Guard infantry, twenty-three regiments of line infantry, two regiments of Guard cavalry, four regiments of line cavalry, three regiments of artillery, one regiment of engineers, forty battalions of reserve infantry and eighty squadrons of reserve cavalry. All the regiments of infantry had four battalions each, and their cannon infantry were detached to form the three new regiments of artillery. The latter had twelve companies each and were equipped with various kinds of guns (light artillery, medium artillery and heavy artillery). The units of Guard cavalry were regiments on paper only, since each of them was just squadron-sized. The regiments of line cavalry were all dragoons, whose members were equipped with carbines, whereas those of the Guard were lancer corps. The active army consisted of volunteers, while the Redeef units were made up of conscripts who could be called to serve in case of military emergency.

The army of 1840–53

Mahmud II died in 1839 and was succeeded as Sultan by Abdulmejid I, a great reformer who initiated a new era of modernization inside the Ottoman Empire that became known as the *Tanzimat*, or Reorganization. The main aim of the new Sultan was to secure the territorial integrity of the Ottoman Empire against both internal nationalist movements and external aggressions. During his long reign, Abdulmejid I carried out several constitutional reforms, some of which achieved great success. Among them was the military reform that introduced conscription, which was part of a wider modernization of the Ottoman public institutions. The war with Egypt of 1839–41 showed the limits of the Nizam-i-Cedit, which was still too small and too concentrated around Constantinople to provide an effective defence of Ottoman lands. In 1843, the New Army was greatly expanded and the territory of the Ottoman Empire was divided into five military regions, each of which was to be garrisoned by an independent army corps. The 1st Army Corps, or Imperial Guard Corps, was based at Constantinople, the 2nd Army Corps at Scutari (Albania), the 3rd Army Corps at Monastir (Macedonia), the 4th Army Corps at Kharpout (Anatolia) and the 5th Army Corps at Damascus (Syria). The 1st and 3rd Army Corps each consisted of the following units: seven regiments of line infantry, four battalions of light infantry, five regiments of cavalry and one regiment of artillery. The other three army corps each comprised six regiments of line infantry, six battalions of light infantry, four regiments of cavalry and one regiment of artillery. Consequently, the whole Ottoman Army now comprised thirty-two regiments of line infantry, twenty-six battalions of light infantry, twenty-two regiments of cavalry and five regiments of artillery. Two of the 1st Army Corps' line infantry regiments belonged to the Imperial Guard; these, like the other thirty regiments, comprised three battalions each. The greatest innovation introduced by the reorganization of 1843 was the battalions of light infantry or *seshaneci* (foot chasseurs). These were equipped with flintlock carbines and were trained to operate on broken terrain, having a higher degree of mobility compared with the line infantrymen. The battalions of *seshaneci* were formed by selecting one-in-eight of the most mobile and skilled soldiers from each line infantry battalion. Until 1843, the light infantry of the Ottoman Army had been entirely made up of irregular mercenaries (*bashi-bazouks*) recruited from different areas of the empire.

Of the twenty-two regiments of cavalry, only two were part of the Imperial Guard and were assigned to the 1st Army Corps. These – whose members were equipped with lances – were known as the 1st or Red Regiment and the 2nd or Blue Regiment because of the distinctive colours of their uniforms. The fifteen regiments of line cavalry were all structured on six squadrons; the first two of the squadrons were equipped with carbines, while the remaining four had lances. The only exception to this rule was the 1st Lancer Regiment of the 1st Army Corps, which had the status of an elite unit and whose squadrons were all armed with lances. Each of the artillery regiments consisted of eleven field companies/batteries manning six field pieces each, plus one mountain company/battery manning four mountain pieces. In addition to the units belonging to the various army corps, the newly created Grand Master of the Artillery commanded the following reserve units that were available for use in every corner of the empire: one regiment of artillery, one regiment of fortress artillery and two regiments of engineers. The regiments of artillery and fortress artillery had twelve companies each, while

Ottoman soldier of the 2nd Foot Regiment (Blue Regiment) of the Imperial Guard.

Uniforms of the Ottoman Army in 1854 (from left to right): cavalryman, foreign instructor with non-regulation patrol jacket, line infantryman and artilleryman. All the uniforms were dark blue, with different facing colours. All the Ottoman regular soldiers had a red fez as headgear.

the regiments of engineers had two battalions each and could be assembled together to form a single brigade.

The Redeef, being formed of reservists who served one month every year, had a territorial organization. Each district of the Ottoman Empire was to provide one regiment of reserve infantry with four battalions plus between one and four squadrons of reserve cavalry (according to its population). In 1848, the first conscription law was

The Ottoman Army

Uniforms of the Ottoman Army in 1854 (from left to right): artilleryman and two infantrymen. In 1839, the Ottomans adopted the single-breasted coatee worn by the artilleryman as the standard uniform of their regular foot troops; with the new dress regulations of 1853, however, the infantry was given the new French-style single-breasted tunic, worn here by the infantrymen.

promulgated in the Ottoman Empire, according to which each conscript (selected by draft) was to serve for five years in the Nizam-i-Cedit and for seven years in the Redeef. Christians and the inhabitants of Constantinople were exempt from compulsory military service. During 1848, a 7th Army Corps was created, based in Iraq and consisting of four regiments of line infantry, four battalions of light infantry, two regiments of cavalry and one regiment of artillery.

It was with the general structure described above that the Ottoman Army entered into the Crimean War in 1853. Before that year, however, some minor alterations were made to the internal organization of the units: the rank of flag-bearer was abolished; a secretary and a second lieutenant were added to the staff of each line infantry regiment; each cavalry regiment received a small regimental staff consisting of one first lieutenant, one second lieutenant and one sergeant-major; and each artillery regiment received a small regimental staff consisting of one second lieutenant and one third lieutenant. The infantry regiments of the Redeef also received their own staff, which comprised the following elements: one colonel, one major, one intendant, one adjutant-major and one secretary-major, plus one secretary for each of the four battalions. In order to facilitate the development of a stronger *esprit de corps* in each unit, all the regiments of the New Army were allotted a band with eighty musicians (continuing an ancient tradition that dated back to the glory days of the Janissaries). Abdulmejid I worked hard from 1846 to improve the general quality of his officers, fixing the standards of the Military Academy and creating four new military colleges. He also established the Council of the Grand Master of the Artillery, which was divided into a War Department and a Testing Department. The War Department supervised the supply of ammunitions to the various units in case of war, while the Testing Department tested new modern weapons imported from overseas in view of their possible future adoption by the Ottoman Army. The Ottoman cavalry was expanded in 1848 with the formation of two new regiments, both of which were attached to the 3rd Army Corps: the Cossack Regiment and the Mounted Chasseurs Regiment. The Cossack Regiment was recruited from Polish political refugees and Zaporozhian Cossacks, but was extremely short-lived, while the Mounted Chasseurs Regiment continued to exist until the outbreak of the Crimean War and consisted of a carabineer regiment, its members (most of whom were Polish exiles) all equipped with carbines.

In addition to the Nizam-i-Cedit and the Redeef, Sultan Abdulmejid I could also count on a small Naval Infantry Corps and a large Gendarmerie Corps. The Naval Infantry Corps, whose members were known as *galeonjees*, received a westernized organization in 1804 when it was structured on two small regiments with 500 marines each. The Gendarmerie Corps was mostly recruited from the sailors of Constantinople, and its members were permitted to sleep with their families at night during times of peace. Under Abdulmejid I, the Naval Infantry Corps was reorganized as a single battalion with 500 *galeonjees* but remained part of the Ottoman Navy and not of the Army. The Ottoman Gendarmes, or *zaptiye*, were created in 1846 and acted as a paramilitary mounted police. Each *eyalet* or region of the Ottoman Empire had a brigade of Gendarmes, the only exception to this rule being Constantinople, which had three brigades. Each province had a company of *zaptiye* and each department a detachment. In the event of war, a good number of the 30,000 Turkish mounted policemen could be mobilized and be brigaded together to form an effective cavalry force.

The army of 1854–56

The early events of the Crimean War clearly showed that the Nizam-i-Cedit was no match for the Russian Army. As a result, under strong pressure from their British and French allies to do so, the Ottomans decided to reorganize and retrain part of both their regular and irregular forces. When hostilities commenced, in order to have enough men to face the Russians, the Turks had no choice but to recruit a large number of irregular mercenaries: the famous *bashi-bazouks* (also known as 'crazy heads'). The latter were raised only in times of war, did not receive pay or uniforms from the government, used every kind of weapon that they could find and were motivated to fight only by expectations of plunder. Most of the *bashi-bazouks* fought on foot, but a number of them could also act as fast-moving light cavalry. They were recruited from all the ethnic groups living inside the Ottoman Empire, but the majority of them were Albanians or Circassians. Since they had their own leaders and officers, these mercenaries were infamous for their indiscipline and for preying on civilian communities. Their irregular style of fighting, consisting of skirmishings and ambushes, was extremely violent; the *bashi-bazouks* were noted for their brutality and had no qualms about committing atrocities to terrorize the enemy. After arriving with their military contingents in the Ottoman Empire, both the British and French tried to 'regularize' the hordes of *bashi-bazouks* who had decided to fight against the Russians. To do this, they proposed to the Ottoman authorities to substitute the local chiefs of the various mercenary groups (known as *sergerdes*) with regular officers from their own expeditionary corps. The French assembled a number of mounted *bashi-bazouks* from Syria and Kurdistan, organizing them – on 24 June 1854 – into a short-lived semi-regular corps known as the Spahis d'Orient. In Algeria, the French had previously created some excellent units of Spahis native cavalry, and now wanted to export their organizational pattern to the Levant. They therefore gave command

Ottoman soldiers photographed at the beginning of the Crimean War. The men with short tunics and white summer trousers are artillerymen, while those with long tunic are infantrymen. The cavalry have tunics with frontal frogging, while the individuals wearing the kolpak are from the 1st Cossack (Polish) Regiment.

of the new Spahis d'Orient to General Yousouf, a Corsican who had embraced Islam several years before and had become known as the 'father' of the Algerian Spahis. Yousouf was tasked with raising eight regiments of mounted *bashi-bazouks* with four squadrons each, but in the end only six weak regiments could be organized. Each of these regiments had one squadron of Syrians, one squadron of Albanians, one squadron of Kurds and one squadron of Turkomans. In August 1854, however, the Spahis d'Orient were disbanded without having seen any fighting, most of them having already deserted soon after they received new weapons from their French officers and NCOs.

During the Crimean War, the Ottomans created some new military units that were made up of Polish soldiers. The Poles had been struggling with the Russians since 1830 in an attempt to restore the independence of their nation, and thus were happy to enlist in any foreign army that was at war with their mortal enemies. The historical phenomenon of the Polish military diaspora is known as the *Wielka Emigracja*, or 'Great Emigration', since it involved a substantial number of men who left their homeland to fight in the ranks of foreign armies. In late 1853, a Polish

The Ottoman Army   175

Polish trooper of the 1st Cossack Regiment in Ottoman service. The black kolpak and dark blue tunic with cutaway sleeves are typically Polish; the waistcoat worn under the tunic is red and the trousers are dark blue with red side-stripe. The flag is the traditional one of the Zaporozhian Cossacks.

patriot and exile named Michal Czajkowski (later known as Sadik Pasha) was tasked by the Turkish authorities with raising a new Cossack regiment from the Slavic Christians who lived in the lands of the Ottoman Empire and from the Cossacks of northern Dobruja. An increasing number of Polish exiles had crossed the borders of the Ottoman lands in recent years, and had even established a logistical base south of the Danube, known as the 'Eastern Agency' (the creation of which had been sponsored by British and French agents). As a result of this situation, Czajkowski, after converting to Islam, was able to raise the 1st Cossack Regiment as the first unit of a larger 'Christian Army' that he was planning to create within the Ottoman Empire. The new regiment consisted of five regular squadrons of lancers and one irregular squadron of Cossacks (another two incomplete Cossack squadrons were added at a later date). The unit was given elegant uniforms and the old banner of the Zaporozhian Cossacks, and against all expectations it fought well on several occasions. The Ottomans had a very small force of cavalry with which to counter the excellent Cossack formations of the Russians, so they sponsored the creation of new Polish units during the course of the Crimean War. A 2nd Cossack Regiment, initially also known as the Polish Legion, was formed in 1854 by Count Wladyslaw Zamoyski, followed by a 3rd Cossack Regiment that was raised in 1855. The two new units, however, were not of the same quality as the first one, and were both disbanded after only a few months of service. In the autumn of 1855, all the Polish cavalry serving in the Ottoman Army were reorganized as a Cossack Brigade of 2,000 men. This new corps, largely equipped and paid for by the British and the French, never saw combat and was disbanded in July 1856. During 1856, for just a few months, the British and French organized a Cossack Division of their own by raising a large number of Polish exiles. This strong corps – some 4,000 men – consisted of the following units: one regiment of line infantry, one regiment of light infantry, one regiment of lancers, one regiment of mounted chasseurs (carabiniers), one battery of foot artillery and one battery of mounted artillery. With the end of the Crimean War, the Cossack Division was disbanded after having never seen active service. In 1857, during the reorganization of the Ottoman Army that followed the Crimean War, the Ottomans decided to re-raise their Cossack Brigade under the command of Sadik Pasha. The reconstituted corps consisted of two regiments with four squadrons each: the Cossack Regiment and the Dragoon Regiment, both of which were given Guard status. Between 1857 and 1865, the Cossack Brigade was mostly employed in patrolling the Ottoman border with Greece and in fighting local bands of brigands. In 1865 the Dragoon Regiment was disbanded and the Cossack Brigade ceased to exist; the Cossack Regiment was retained in service as part of the Imperial Guard until it was destroyed during the early phase of the Russo-Turkish War of 1877–78.

The regional contingents

Some regions of the Ottoman Empire enjoyed a high degree of autonomy and had their own independent armies, which could support Turkish forces in the event of war but could also revolt against them when there was the opportunity to fight for the full independence of their homeland. In total there were six of such autonomous regional armies: the Egyptian Army, the Tunisian Army, the Serbian Army, the Montenegrin Army, the Moldavian Army and the Wallachian Army. Only the Egyptian and Tunisian armies participated in the Crimean War, providing some expeditionary contingents to the Ottomans, with all the others remaining neutral. In 1854, the Egyptian Army, which had been remodelled and westernized several years before the Ottoman reformation, consisted of the following units: twenty regiments of line infantry, one regiment of Guard cavalry, ten regiments of line cavalry (equipped with lances), three regiments of artillery and two battalions of engineers. Of these, nine regiments of line infantry, one squadron of Guard cavalry, two regiments of line cavalry and one-and-a-half regiments of artillery were sent to fight against the Russians in the Crimean War. The regiment of Guard cavalry, consisting of three squadrons, was an elite unit, its members – equipped with helmets and cuirasses – known as *zirkhagi* ('iron men'). The westernized Tunisian Army originated during late 1830, following the French conquest of Algiers, when Hussayn Bey – the ruler of Tunisia – decided that a modern army had to be organized in his country as soon as possible to face an eventual French attack against Tunis.

Line infantryman of the Egyptian contingent fighting in the Crimean War. The general appearance is very similar to that of the Ottoman soldiers, except for the small turban wrapped around the fez.

By 1854, the Tunisian Army consisted of the following units: seven regiments of line infantry with three battalions of eight companies each, one regiment of cavalry with four squadrons and four regiments of artillery with three battalions of eight companies each. In addition to these units, there was a regiment of naval infantry, a small mounted Bey's Bodyguard, three corps of Spahis irregular cavalry and several auxiliary foot units recruited from the warlike Zwawa tribes (who had always provided excellent soldiers for the rulers of Tunis). The Tunisian expeditionary force that took part in the Crimean War consisted of 7,000 men, with six infantry battalions, one cavalry regiment and two field batteries with six guns each. The Serbian and Montenegrin armies of 1854 were very small, the former consisting of two infantry battalions, one cavalry squadron and one field battery, while the latter comprised a Guard of the Prince with 400 chosen soldiers and forty independent companies of semi-regular infantry. The armies of the Danubian Principalities, which were under a strong Russian influence, were also quite small in 1854. The Moldavian Army had one regiment of infantry with three battalions, one lancer regiment with two squadrons and one field battery, while that of Wallachia had three regiments of infantry with two battalions each, two lancer squadrons, one field battery and half a mounted battery.

Albanian *bashi-bazouk* in Ottoman service. The Albanian irregulars serving in the Ottoman and Egyptian military as mercenaries were usually dressed in green and wore a national costume that was quite similar to that of the Greek mountaineers.

Chapter 5

The Piedmontese Army

The Piedmontese Army was the main military driving force of the Risorgimento, or Italian Unification. It was the only military force in Italy to have a high level of professionalism and the same standards of service as the armies of the other European powers. The army was a perfect mirror of Piedmontese society, being generally conservative but at the same time interested in innovations. The reign of King Charles Albert (1831–49) was a period of fundamental importance for the army of Piedmont – also known as the Kingdom of Sardinia – which underwent a gradual but radical process of transformation and modernization. With the great reforms of 1832, the Piedmontese Army adopted a mixed system of recruitment based on both the French and Prussian models: around a core of 16,000 professional soldiers serving for eight years, the armed forces also included a levy of 8,000 provincial conscripts who served for just fourteen months. The war of 1848–49 with Austria, however, ended with a disastrous defeat for the Kingdom of Sardinia, despite its armed forces performing well during the first part of the conflict. In the ten years following their rout at the Battle of Novara, the Piedmontese Army acquired more combat experience through its participation in the Crimean War and gradually improved its quality thanks to the reforms of its new Minister of War, Alfonso La Marmora. The period of service for the conscripts was lengthened to four or six years, depending on the branch of service. The total number of soldiers was increased to 75,000 and the quantity of light infantry and light cavalry units was expanded. The Piedmontese intervention in the Crimean War was financed by Britain with a loan of £1 million, and the Royal Navy agreed to transport the Piedmontese contingent to the theatre of war on board its ships. The Piedmontese decided to send an army corps of 15,000 soldiers, which was to maintain the same number of men thanks to the continuous shipment of reinforcements from Italy. Command of the Piedmontese Expeditionary Corps was given to General Alfonso La Marmora, the best commander of the Sardinian Army and the founder of the famous Bersaglieri light infantry corps. The Piedmontese eventually sent 18,000 men to Crimea, who arrived in the theatre of operations in May 1855. The line infantry and cavalry units were drawn from soldiers who had volunteered for the expedition, whereas the Bersaglieri, artillery, sappers and train were dispatched direct from their units. Thanks to its participation in the Crimean War, Piedmont formed a military alliance with Napoleon III's France and defeated the Austrians in 1859. By 1861, the Piedmontese had completed the unification of Italy thanks to the superiority of their armed forces.

Infantry

According to a table of organization issued on 4 May 1839, the Piedmontese infantry was structured on ten brigades: the Brigata Guardie (Guard Brigade) plus nine line brigades (the Savoia, Piemonte, Aosta, Cuneo, La Regina, Casale, Pinerolo, Savona and Acqui). The Guard Brigade was formed with one regiment of grenadiers and one of *cacciatori* (light infantry), both of them being structured on two battalions of grenadiers and one of *cacciatori*, with four companies each. The line brigades each had two regiments of line infantry, for a total of eighteen infantry regiments. Each regiment of line infantry was structured on three battalions: the first and second with one company of grenadiers and three of fusiliers, the third with four companies of light infantry. Each company comprised 250 men. In case of mobilization for war, a fourth battalion with four companies of fusiliers was added to each regiment. With the outbreak of the war with Austria in 1848, the fourth battalions of each line regiment were soon formed, and twelve of these depot battalions were eventually assembled to form four new provisional regiments of line infantry, grouped into two new autonomous brigades. At the end of the 1848 campaign, these four provisional regiments and the six independent depot battalions were disbanded, their soldiers being sent back to reinforce their original units.

The Piedmontese infantry then underwent a major reorganization. The cadres of the disbanded units, together with new recruits, formed two reserve battalions for each line infantry regiment. The first of these two battalions was to perform fighting roles and was formed by more expert soldiers, while the second battalion had functions of internal security or performed auxiliary roles. After the Austrian reconquest of Lombardy, the military units organized by the Lombard patriots were absorbed into the Piedmontese Army and were used to form four new line infantry regiments. On 14 October 1848, the Guard Brigade was also reorganized: it was now to be structured on two regiments of grenadiers and one of *cacciatori*, the grenadier regiments having two battalions each and the regiment of *cacciatori* four battalions. On 16 October, four new provisional regiments of infantry were formed using twelve of the 'first-line' reserve battalions. On 27 October, the strength all the line infantry companies was reduced from 250 to 180 men. On 11 November, a new regiment of infantry, the 23rd, was formed with four battalions: the first and second battalions were composed respectively of volunteers coming from Parma and Modena, while the third and fourth were made up of Piedmontese new recruits. On 6 February 1849, all the original eighteen line infantry regiments again formed their fourth battalions. On 9 February, another five new provisional regiments of infantry were formed, bringing the total number of these units to nine. One of these new regiments was formed with the four reserve battalions of the two grenadier regiments from the Guard Brigade. On 11 March, the Piedmontese infantry was again totally reorganized. The 19th and

Piedmontese soldiers of the Guard Brigade, with *cacciatore* (light infantryman) on the left and *granatieri* (grenadiers) on the right. The *cacciatori* had a black shako as headgear, while the *granatieri* wore a massive bearskin that is still used today with parade dress. On the right are an officer and a drummer.

Piedmontese sergeant of the Guard Grenadiers (left) and private of the Guard Chasseurs (right). Both have the additional white lace of the Guard Brigade on the collar and cuffs. The two figures are wearing the M1842 double-breasted tunic, which had coloured shoulder rolls.

The Piedmontese Army

Piedmontese corporal of a line infantry brigade, wearing the M1842 uniform. He is from a light company, as shown by the green colour of the shoulder rolls and shako's pompom, as well as by the brass badge of his headgear.

20th Infantry Regiments formed the new 1st Lombard Brigade, while the 21st and 22nd Infantry Regiments made up the new 2nd Lombard Brigade. Both brigades were assembled together to form a Lombard Division. The first four provisional regiments were transformed into regular ormations, numbered the 24th, 25th, 26th and 27th. The provisional regiment formed from the grenadiers of the Guard Brigade became the 3rd Grenadiers of the Guard, while the 5th and 6th provisional regiments of line infantry became the new 28th and 29th Regiments of Infantry; these three regiments were grouped together in the Provisional Reserve Division. The 7th and 8th provisional regiments became the new 30th and 31st Regiments of Infantry. The fourth battalions of the original eighteen line infantry regiments were now used to form six new infantry regiments with three battalions each. These new regiments were numbered 32–37.

After the end of the First Italian War of Unification, the Piedmontese infantry was significantly reduced in numbers, again adopting the original organization that it had before the war: eighteen line infantry regiments structured on nine brigades, plus three regiments of the Guard (two of grenadiers and one of *cacciatori*). All the new units which had been formed during the conflict were

Piedmontese NCO (left) and drummer (right) of the line infantry, wearing the new M1849 tunic that was used during the Crimean War. The new tunic was single-breasted and had coloured cuff flaps. It was adopted together with the simpler model of shako shown here.

disbanded. On 12 October 1849, the internal structure of the line regiments was modified, reducing the strength of each unit from four to three active battalions. Each battalion now had six companies: one elite company, four line companies and one depot company. On 20 April 1850, the Guard Brigade was disbanded, being replaced by a new Grenadier Brigade formed from the two regiments of grenadiers, while the regiment of *cacciatori* acted as an independent unit (being renamed the Cacciatori di Sardegna). On 19 March 1852, this structure was changed again, with the Cacciatori di Sardegna being absorbed into the Grenadier Brigade (which comprised two regiments of grenadiers). At the same time the internal structure of the line regiments was also modified, with individual battalions now comprising just four active companies.

Until 1831, the Piedmontese Army had included a number of independent light infantry units, but in that year the units of *cacciatori* were disbanded and the duties of the light troops were transferred to the line infantry. Nevertheless, it was soon clear to certain of the Piedmontese generals that a separate corps of light infantry was vitally needed. This situation lasted until 1836, when the new corps of the Bersaglieri was formed by Alessandro La Marmora. Initially it faced many difficulties and the diffidence of the more conservative Piedmontese generals. Despite this, the first company of Bersaglieri soon reached a high level of professionalism, undergoing innovative training and being equipped with rifled carbines of the La Marmora type (invented by their commander). A second and third company were later created, and in 1843 all three units were grouped to form a battalion. A fourth company was added some time later. With the outbreak of the First Italian War of Unification, the corps of the Bersaglieri was expanded with the formation of a second battalion, having four companies like the original one. On 21 November 1848, a third battalion was added as a result of the excellent performance by the Bersaglieri during the campaign of that year. There was a further expansion on 30 December, with a fourth and a fifth battalion being created, again with four companies each. The Bersaglieri became an example for all the Italian units of light infantry due to their great mobility and reputation as excellent marksmen. Many of the units of volunteers which were formed during the First Italian War of Unification adopted their fighting style and peculiar uniform, as well as various regular formations of other Italian armies. Soon after the war of 1848–49, three further battalions were added, then in March 1850 the 9th Battalion was formed, while the 10th was created on 19 March 1852.

Piedmontese Bersagliere light infantryman, with M1842 tunic. The most distinctive elements of the Piedmontese light infantry's outfit were the green cords-and-flounders and the *vaira* wide-brimmed hat with capercaillie feathers.

Cavalry

According to the organization established on 18 November 1841, the Piedmontese mounted units comprised six regiments of line cavalry that each had six squadrons. On 12 September 1848, three squadrons of guides were added to the existing units to act at the orders of the various military commands. During the 1848 campaign, the Piedmontese cavalry operated alongside two units formed by the revolutionary Provisional Government of Milan: a regiment of dragoons and one of *cavalleggeri*

Piedmontese line cavalrymen. Their uniforms, like all the others of the Piedmontese forces, have Austrian cut but French colours. Note the white Savoy cross reproduced on the front of the helmet.

Piedmontese trooper of the light cavalry. The *cavalleggeri* regiments were created in 1850 and their members were dressed quite similarly to the line cavalrymen except for their headgear.

(light cavalrymen). These two corps followed the retreat of the Piedmontese Army and were reorganized in September 1848; the dragoons were structured on six squadrons, the *cavalleggeri* on two. On 14 May 1849, the regiment of *cavalleggeri* was disbanded and that of dragoons was transformed into the new 7th Regiment of Line Cavalry. After the campaign of 1849, a special military commission was created to analyse and understand the reasons for the defeat. According to the conclusions of the commission, one of the reasons had been the total lack of light cavalry units. As a consequence, on 3 January 1850, the Piedmontese cavalry was totally reorganized with the formation of new *cavalleggeri* units. Under the new structure, the line cavalry was reduced to four regiments and five new regiments of *cavalleggeri* were created, while the three squadrons of guides were disbanded. All nine regiments now had four active squadrons and one depot squadron.

Artillery and technical corps

On 7 January 1845, the Piedmontese artillery was structured on six brigades with two batteries each. The 1st Brigade was the only mounted one, while the 6th comprised two positional batteries. In January 1848, the artillery forces were increased with the creation of three new batteries: one of mounted artillery, one of field artillery and one of positional artillery. In May of the same year, the 10th Field Battery was formed, which later replaced the 4th Field Battery that had been transformed into the 4th Positional Battery. In March 1849, shortly before the second campaign of the war with Austria, a new 10th Field Battery was formed. Another four provisional batteries were also added: one from Modena and three from Lombardy (two field batteries and a positional battery). In addition to the batteries, the Piedmontese artillery had a brigade of artillery workers and one of pontoniers (on two companies). On 1 October 1850, the Piedmontese artillery was totally reorganized on three regiments: the 1st Regiment of Artillery Workers, 2nd Regiment of Garrison Artillery and 3rd Regiment of Field Artillery. The Regiment of Artillery Workers comprised two brigades, one of regular artillery workers and one of pontoniers. The Regiment of Garrison Artillery was structured on two brigades, with six companies each, while the Regiment of Field Artillery was organized on one mounted brigade with two batteries and six field brigades with three batteries each. According to the organization established on 22 April 1843, the Piedmontese *zappatori* (Engineers) were organized into a single battalion having four companies (one of miners and three of sappers). A depot company was added five years later. On 29 September 1848, the unit was expanded and became a regiment with two battalions, each having an elite company of miners and four companies of sappers. On 12 October 1849, the fourth companies of sappers were disbanded in both of the battalions. In 1852, the strength of the two battalions was increased to five companies each. Before the war of 1848, the Piedmontese train was organized on five divisions, each with four sections. It was expanded to fourteen divisions for the campaign of 1849, with a total of fifty-six sections. At the end of the war, the number of divisions were initially reduced to six, then on 12 December 1852 the train was reduced to just four companies.

From its foundation in 1814, the famous corps of the Carabinieri Reali (Royal Carabineers) acted as the royal gendarmerie of the Kingdom of Sardinia and the mounted guard of the Piedmontese kings. The Royal Carabineers was composed of foot as well as mounted units. In times of war, contingents of Carabinieri were usually mobilized and attached to the army on campaign. With the outbreak of the First Italian War of Unification, three squadrons of mounted Carabinieri (some 430 men in total) were mobilized to act as the personal guard for King Charles Albert. A further three half-squadrons were attached to the various divisions to act as military police. In 1852, the whole corps was reorganized on seven divisions (the Torino,

Piedmontese gunner of the horse artillery (left), officer of the horse artillery (centre) and private of the sappers (right). The horse artillery had a distinctive extra-long plume on the shako, while the *zappatori* had a strange headgear consisting of a shako with a wide brim.

The Piedmontese Army 191

Piedmontese NCO (left) and officer (right) of the naval infantry. Their general appearance is very similar to that of the line infantry, except for the peculiar badge worn on the front of the shako.

Savoia, Alessandria, Genova, Cuneo, Novara and Nizza). In Sardinia, the functions of the Carabinieri were performed by another police corps, the Cavalleggeri di Sardegna (Light Cavalrymen of Sardinia). This was a cavalry regiment with three squadrons, each of which were divided into three smaller divisions. On 21 April 1852, after a failed mutiny, the unit was disbanded and substituted with the new Carabinieri of Sardinia, organized on two divisions (the Cagliari and Sassari).

The Piedmontese Navy included a battalion of naval infantry known as the Battaglione Real Navi. According to its organization established in 1830, the unit had eight companies for a total of 958 men. In March 1848, a detachment of naval infantry was sent to the front to join the land forces in the First Italian War of Unification. On 8 April 1850, the battalion was transformed into the Regiment Real Navi with the creation of a second battalion. However, this structure did not last for long: on 26 March 1851, the unit was reduced back to a single battalion with 500 men in six companies.

The order of battle of the Piedmontese Expeditionary Corps sent to Crimea was as follows:

1st Infantry Division

2nd Brigade
2nd Provisional Regiment: 1st Battalion (with troops from the 3rd Infantry Regiment), 2nd Battalion (4th Infantry Regiment), 3rd Battalion (15th Infantry Regiment) and 4th Battalion (16th Infantry Regiment).
2nd Bersaglieri Battalion: 9th Bersaglieri Company (from the 3rd Bersaglieri Battalion), 10th Bersaglieri Company (3rd Bersaglieri Battalion), 13th Bersaglieri Company (4th Bersaglieri Battalion) and 14th Bersaglieri Company (4th Bersaglieri Battalion).
7th Field Artillery Battery

3rd Brigade
3rd Provisional Regiment: 1st Battalion (with troops from the 7th Infantry Regiment), 2nd Battalion (8th Infantry Regiment), 3rd Battalion (13th Infantry Regiment) and 4th Battalion (14th Infantry Regiment).
3rd Bersaglieri Battalion: 17th Bersaglieri Company (from the 5th Bersaglieri Battalion), 18th Bersaglieri Company (5th Bersaglieri Battalion), 21st Bersaglieri Company (6th Bersaglieri Battalion) and 22nd Bersaglieri Company (6th Bersaglieri Battalion).
10th Field Artillery Battery

2nd Infantry Division

4th Brigade
<u>4th Provisional Regiment</u>: 1st Battalion (with troops from the 9th Infantry Regiment), 2nd Battalion (10th Infantry Regiment), 3rd Battalion (15th Infantry Regiment) and 4th Battalion (16th Infantry Regiment).
<u>4th Bersaglieri Battalion</u>: 25th Bersaglieri Company (from the 7th Bersaglieri Battalion), 26th Bersaglieri Company (7th Bersaglieri Battalion), 29th Bersaglieri Company (8th Bersaglieri Battalion) and 30th Bersaglieri Company (8th Bersaglieri Battalion).
<u>13th Field Artillery Battery</u>

5th Brigade
<u>5th Provisional Regiment</u>: 1st Battalion (with troops from the 11th Infantry Regiment), 2nd Battalion (12th Infantry Regiment), 3rd Battalion (17th Infantry Regiment) and 4th Battalion (18th Infantry Regiment).
<u>5th Bersaglieri Battalion</u>: 33rd Bersaglieri Company (from the 9th Bersaglieri Battalion), 34th Bersaglieri Company (9th Bersaglieri Battalion), 37th Bersaglieri Company (10th Bersaglieri Battalion) and 38th Bersaglieri Company (10th Bersaglieri Battalion).
<u>16th Field Artillery Battery</u>

Reserve Forces

Reserve Brigade
<u>1st Provisional Regiment</u>: 1st Battalion (with troops from the 1st Grenadier Regiment), 2nd Battalion (2nd Grenadier Regiment), 3rd Battalion (1st Infantry Regiment) and 4th Battalion (2nd Infantry Regiment).
<u>1st Bersaglieri Battalion</u>: 1st Bersaglieri Company (from the 1st Bersaglieri Battalion), 2nd Bersaglieri Company (1st Bersaglieri Battalion), 5th Bersaglieri Company (2nd Bersaglieri Battalion) and 6th Bersaglieri Company (2nd Bersaglieri Battalion).
<u>Reserve Artillery Brigade</u>: 1st Field Artillery Battery, 4th Field Artillery Battery.

Provisional Light Cavalry Regiment
1st Squadron (with troops from the Cavalleggeri di Novara Regiment).
2nd Squadron (Cavalleggeri di Aosta Regiment).
3rd Squadron (Cavalleggeri di Saluzzo Regiment).

4th Squadron (Cavalleggeri di Monferrato Regiment).
5th Squadron (Cavalleggeri di Alessandria Regiment).

Provisional Fortress Artillery Battalion
1st Fortress Artillery Battery (from the 1st Fortress Artillery Brigade).
2nd Fortress Artillery Battery (1st Fortress Artillery Brigade)
7th Fortress Artillery Battery (2nd Fortress Artillery Brigade).
8th Fortress Artillery Battery (2nd Fortress Artillery Brigade).

Mixed Artillery Workers Company

Provisional Sapper Battalion
1st Sapper Company (from the Sapper Regiment).
2nd Sapper Company (Sapper Regiment).
6th Sapper Company (Sapper Regiment).
7th Sapper Company (Sapper Regiment).

Army Train
1st Army Train Company.
2nd Army Train Company.

Carabinieri Detachment (fifty men acting as military police).

Bibliography

Ales, Stefano, *Dall'Armata Sarda all'Esercito Italiano 1843–1861* (Ufficio Storico dello Stato Maggiore dell'Esercito, 1990).
Anonymous, *Observations on the Turkish Contingent* (Smith, 1856).
Barthorp, Michael, *The British Army on Campaign: the Crimea, 1854–1856* (Osprey Publishing, 1987).
Bayley, C.C., *Mercenaries for the Crimea: the German, Swiss and Italian Legions in British Service 1854–1856* (Queen's University Press, 1977).
Chappell, Mike, *Redcaps: Britain's Military Police* (Osprey Publishing, 1997).
Delpérier, Louis, *L'Armée de Napoléon III* (Editions du Coteau, 2011).
Devautour, P. and Huré, R., *L'Armée d'Afrique 1830–1962* (Lavauzelle, 1980).
Esposito, Gabriele, *Armies of the Italian Wars of Unification, 1848–1870: Piedmont and the Two Sicilies* (Osprey Publishing, 2017).
Fahmy, Khaled, *All the Pasha's Men: Mehmed Ali, his army and the making of modern Egypt* (University of Cairo Press, 2002).
Flaherty, Chris, *The Sardinian Expeditionary Corps* (Soldiershop Publishing, 2021).
Flaherty, Chris, *Turkish Crimean War Uniforms* (self-published, 2020).
Glogowski, P. and de Gmeline, P., *Histoire des Spahis 1834–1918* (Editions Le Triomphe, 2018).
Jouineau, André, *L'Armée de Napoleon III* (Editions Heimdal, 2018).
Jovic, T. and Jovicevic, M., *The Montenegrin Army: Organisation and Uniforms* (Nasljede, 2006).
La Sabretache, *Les Chasseurs d'Afrique 1831–1964* (Carnets de La Sabretache, 1974).
La Sabretache, *Les Joyeux* (Carnets de La Sabretache, 1979).
La Sabretache, *Les Spahis* (Carnets de La Sabretache, 1982).
La Sabretache, *Les Zouaves* (Carnets de La Sabretache, 1985).
La Sabretache, *Tirailleurs Algériens et Tunisiens 1830–1964* (Carnets de La Sabretache, 1980).
Mollo, Boris, *Uniforms of the Imperial Russian Army* (Blandford Press, 1979).
Montagnon, Pierre, *L'Armée d'Afrique* (Pygmalion, 2012).
Muzeul Militar National, *Uniformele Armatei Romane 1830–1930* (Marvan, 1930).
Nicholson, J.B.R., *The British Army of the Crimea* (Osprey Publishing, 1974).
Nicolle, David, *Armies of the Ottoman Empire 1775–1820* (Osprey Publishing, 1998).
Pappas, Nicholas Charles, *Greeks in Russian military service in the late XVIII and early XIX centuries* (Institute for Balkan Studies, 1991).
Rosière, Pierre, *Spahis* (Richer/Vilo, 1984).
Roubicek, Marcel, *Early Modern Arab Armies* (Franciscan Press, 1977).
Roubicek, Marcel, *Modern Ottoman Troops 1797–1915 in contemporary pictures* (Franciscan Press, 1978).

Sicard, J. and Vauvillier, F., *Les Chasseurs d'Afrique* (Histoire et Collections, 2008).
Spring, Laurence, *Uniforms of the Russian Army during the Crimean War 1854–1856* (Partizan Press, 2012).
Thomas, Robert H.G., *The Russian Army of the Crimean War 1854–1856* (Osprey Publishing, 1991).
Various authors, *Histoire et épopée des troupes coloniales* (Les Presses Modernes, 1965).
Vasic, Pavle, *Uniforms of the Serbian Army 1808–1918* (Prosveta, 1980).
Viskovatov, A.V., *Historical Description of the Clothing and Arms of the Russian Army, 1825–1855* (Saint Petersburg's Military Typography Office, 1861).
Vladescu, Cristian M., *Uniformele Armatei Romane* (Editura Meridiane, 1977).
Wilkinson-Latham, Robert, *Uniforms and Weapons of the Crimean War* (Harper Collins, 1977).
Windrow, Martin, *French Foreign Legion 1831–1871* (Osprey Publishing, 2016).
Windrow, Martin, *Uniforms of the French Foreign Legion 1831–1981* (Blandford Press, 1981).

Index

Alfonso La Marmora, 179, 185

Battaglione Real Navi, 192

Cacciatori di Sardegna, 185
Cent-gardes Squadron, 77, 79
Company of Palace Grenadiers, 121
Coote Manningham, 19
Cossack Division, 176

Departmental Legions, 81, 90
Duke of Orleans, 82

Finnish Guards' Rifle Battalion, 118

Greek Legion, 162
Guard of the Prince, 178

Heavy Brigade, 32
Hetman Regiment, 130

Jacques Prevost, 16, 17
John Moore, 22

Light Brigade, 36, 39, 102
Louis Philippe, 73, 82

Mounted Pioneers, 135, 144

Naval Brigade, 54

Pierre Bosquet, 36
Polish Legion, 175

Reserve Sapper Battalions, 148
Royal Malta Fencible Regiment, 58
Royal Military Academy, 44

Siberian Division, 150
Spahis d'Orient, 108

William Ferguson Beatson, 67, 72